IMPLOSION

IMPLOSION

THE END OF RUSSIA AND WHAT IT MEANS FOR AMERICA

ILAN BERMAN

REGNERY
Publishing, Inc.

An Eagle Publishing Company • Washington, DC

Cataloging-in-Publication data on file with the Library of Congress

ISBN 978-1-62157-157-5

Published in the United States by
Regnery Publishing, Inc.
One Massachusetts Avenue NW
Washington, DC 20001
www.Regnery.com

Manufactured in the United States of America
10 9 8 7 6 5 4 3 2 1

Books are available in quantity for promotional or premium use. Write to Director of Special Sales, Regnery Publishing, Inc., One Massachusetts Avenue NW, Washington, DC 20001, for information on discounts and terms, or call (202) 216-0600.

Distributed to the trade by
Perseus Distribution
250 West 57th Street
New York, NY 10107

In loving memory of Misha,
my own personal Solzhenitsyn

CONTENTS

Russia: Administrative Divisions

★ National capital
—— Administrative boundary
• Administrative center

Republic
Oblast
Kray
Autonomous okrug
Autonomous oblast

The name of an oblast or kray is shown in white only when the name differs from that of the administrative center. Moscow and Saint Petersburg are federal cities that have the same status as the other 81 administrative divisions.

Administrative divisions listed below are referred to by number on the map.

1 Adygeya
2 Karachayevo-Cherkesiya
3 Kabardino-Balkariya
4 North Ossetia
5 Ingushetiya
6 Chechnya
7 Mordoviya
8 Chuvashiya
9 Mariy-El
10 Udmurtiya

Boundary representation is not necessarily authoritative.

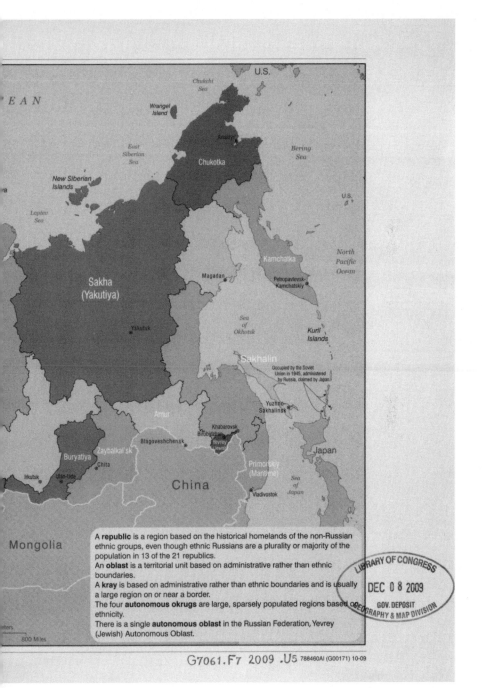

A **republic** is a region based on the historical homelands of the non-Russian ethnic groups, even though ethnic Russians are a plurality or majority of the population in 13 of the 21 republics.
An **oblast** is a territorial unit based on administrative rather than ethnic boundaries.
A **kray** is based on administrative rather than ethnic boundaries and is usually a large region on or near a border.
The four **autonomous okrugs** are large, sparsely populated regions based on ethnicity.
There is a single **autonomous oblast** in the Russian Federation, Yevrey (Jewish) Autonomous Oblast.

G7061.F7 2009 .U5 788460AI (G00171) 10-09

Credit: Library of Congress

FOREWORD

Ian Berman's *Implosion: The End of Russia and What It Means for America* is a very important addition to current efforts to think strategically about America and the world.

In the tradition of Herman Pirchner and the American Foreign Policy Council, it looks at Russia and not merely at its president, Vladimir Putin. The combination of his personality, the disciplined ruthlessness of his KGB background, and the temporary advantage of the energy resources in providing a windfall to the Russian state have enabled Putin to occupy a larger space in international relations than the strategic position of Russia would justify.

In many ways we are all still affected by the scale of the Soviet Empire, its toughness in playing the major role in defeating Nazi Germany despite enormous casualties, and its ability to mobilize 20 percent of the economy to build a military machine out of all proportion to its long term capacity (and, one could argue, ultimately bankrupting the country, as had been suggested would happen in 1950 in National Security Council Report 68).

Russia's relative influence is also helped by its continued possession of one of the world's two largest nuclear arsenals, its relatively modern arms industry, and the sheer geographic expanse of the country. When you look at a map, you instinctively assume a country that big has to count for something.

Finally, Russia still benefits from being one of the five permanent members of the United Nations Security Council. It inevitably, and at virtually no cost to Moscow, is at the center of the dialogue in international negotiations simply by the historic achievement of having been there at the creation, to borrow Dean Acheson's term.

The question Ilan Berman puts on the table is whether Russia is a declining power more like the two weaker permanent members of the Security Council (France and Britain) than a true peer of the United States and China.

There are three great advantages to this incisive study.

First, Berman gets one thinking strategically. Not about this week's posturing in Syria or next week's press event of Putin posing shirtless next to a dead tiger, but rather thinking beyond Putin about the underlying strategic strengths and weaknesses of the current Russian system.

Second, Berman looks to the roots of any nation's long-term power capabilities and examines demography and comparative development. Experts have been warning ever since the collapse of the Soviet Empire that Russia is in a deep demographic crisis. Berman walks the reader through the details, and they are very convincing. Alcoholism, abortion, suicide, and emigration are all combining to shrink the Russian ethnic population. At the same time, the Muslim population of Russia is growing. Muslim Russians don't drink, don't commit suicide, don't have abortions, have many children, and have a much more optimistic view of the future than their ethnic Russian counterparts. As Berman notes, Putin's successors are simply going to have fewer people with a much more difficult ethnic mix to deal with. Russia beyond Putin will inherently be a smaller player on the world stage because it will no longer have the population to be a major one.

This population imbalance will play itself out in two different directions. Internally, the tensions between Muslim and non-Muslim Russians will almost inevitably exacerbate as the energy and youth of the former crowds the aging, declining Russian Christian population. Berman's recounting of the number of mosques being built in Russia today is in itself a convincing insight into the tensions of the future. Externally, the surging Chinese population will almost inevitably lead to massive Chinese involvement in Asiatic Russia where the Russian population is declining. (A side effect of the end of the Soviet totalitarian system is that a lot of people who were compelled to live in bleak, cold areas are now moving to warmer, more modern areas—and the people in those nicer areas are moving out of Russia to Europe and the United States.)

Third, Berman's last decade has been spent studying radical Islam and its terrorist component and he brings that expertise to bear on Russia's internal problems. It isn't just that there will be relatively more Muslims in Russia. The odds are very high that a larger and larger portion of the Muslim population will be attracted to and indoctrinated in a more extreme and more violent aspect of Islam. Because of his unique Russian–Middle Eastern dual specialties, Berman is able to bring together factors many analysts miss.

The primary Russian internal threat is from the radical wing of Sunni Islam. In effect, it is a variant on Wahhabism. This threat is exacerbated by the Russian alliance with the dictatorships in Iran and Syria. Both Russian allies are in the Shi'a camp at a time when the Shi'a-Sunni split may be more bitter and trending toward more violence than any period in recent history. In effect, the Russians may find themselves on the wrong side of an Islamic civil war and that may intensify the efforts outsiders put into radicalizing and militarizing Russia's own domestic Muslim population.

Berman weaves these patterns together with the corruption of the current regime and its impact on capital and foreign investment fleeing the country. The gap between the authoritarian, criminally penetrated, decaying Russia and the Russia that might have evolved is tragic and has consequences both for individual Russians and for American policy.

I remember visiting the collapsing Soviet Union and early post-Soviet Russia in the early 1990s. Again and again everyday people would say to us, "we just want to become a normal country." By that they meant a country with the rule of law, opportunity for everyday folks, and a chance to do better economically over time.

As Berman makes clear, that "normal country" was killed off by the oligarchs, organized crime, and the KGB holdovers. The consequences of that failure will limit Russia's future. That reality should

be the baseline for American thinking about strategic planning dealing with Russia.

—Newt Gingrich
Former Speaker of the House
July 7, 2013

RUSSIA'S DISORDER COMES WEST

On April 15, 2013, two bombs went off on Boylston Street, near the finish line of the famous Boston Marathon. The improvised explosive devices, seemingly timed to go off during peak crowd numbers, ripped through the spectators, killing three and injuring more than 250 others in the largest terrorist incident to take place on U.S. soil since the attacks of 9/11.

In the days that followed, a massive dragnet by law enforcement authorities netted two perpetrators of Chechen extraction: twenty-six-year-old Tamerlan Tsarnaev and his nineteen-year-old brother, Dzhokhar. The resulting showdown left the former dead and the latter hospitalized and awaiting justice in the U.S. legal system.

Speculation has abounded about the motivations that led the two brothers to carry out their brazen act of terror. By all accounts, both were homegrown radicals, albeit ones who had received inspiration, and perhaps even dangerous instruction, from ideologues abroad. But at least in some measure, the roots of the Tsarnaevs' militancy can be traced back to Russia's long-running struggle against radical Islam—a phenomenon that, two decades after the collapse of the USSR, has begun to emerge as a threat to the West.

It is also a foretaste of things to come. Today, the once-mighty Russian state is crumbling under the weight of its own internal contradictions. A rising tide of Islamic radicalism is only one sign of this disorder. Others include population decline on a catastrophic scale, as well as growing strategic competition with neighboring China. As these trends consume Russia, the reverberations will be felt far beyond its borders, including here in the West.

But we should start with a word of caution. History teaches us that nothing is inevitable. Prognosticating about the future is a seductive pastime, and more than a few foreign policy analysts have tried their hands at it over the years. Their track records, however, suggest that such prophesying is an occupation better left to fortune-tellers and clairvoyants.

This book, then, isn't about the certain collapse of Russia. It's easy to imagine that the country might indeed be able to muddle through the coming decades, despite the mounting pressures now taking shape within its borders.

Rather, it's about the end of Russia as we know it. Today, the Russian state is on the cusp of a monumental transformation, brought about by demographic decline, radical (and rapid) ethnic and sectarian change, and a profound shift in the geopolitical balance of power between it and its sometime ally, China. Left unaddressed, these trends will transform the very nature of the Russian state and will do so in ways that will have global implications—including for the United States, which still dominates the Russian imagination as a measure of their own worth and as a strategic adversary.

The changes outlined in the pages that follow could well lead to Russia's outright collapse. However, they might not. One thing is for certain: the Russia that America will have to contend with tomorrow will look very different than the one we see today. Today's Russia is quickly becoming a thing of the past.

CHAPTER ONE

MISREADING RUSSIA

The year is 2040, and Russia is virtually unrecognizable. Decades of population decline and societal malaise have eaten away at the once-mighty Russian state, leaving it a shadow of its former self. Domestically, the country is undergoing a massive social upheaval, as the country's dwindling and increasingly nationalistic Slavic population wages what amounts to a civil "cold war" with an expanding, and radicalizing, Muslim underclass. Separatist tendencies are on the rise in the country's majority-Muslim republics. Some have had to be forcibly prevented from breaking away from the Russian state, while others are planning for just such an exit, despite threats (and payoffs) from Moscow. Violent attacks by domestic Islamist extremists and foreign *jihadists* have become commonplace—scaring away tourists and discouraging foreign investment. Desperate to maintain order, the Russian government has resorted to widespread, sustained repression of a sort not seen since the days of the Soviet Union, further radicalizing the government's political opponents and isolating Russia from the West.

Meanwhile, the territory of the Russian Federation looks dramatically different than it did just twenty years before. Decades of Slavic depopulation and stealthy Chinese immigration have made Beijing the *de facto* overlord of Russia's resource-rich Far East. Russia no longer has any hope of emerging as an Asian political and economic power. China has displaced it, and Russia has tried to compensate with territorial conquest in the post-Soviet space, absorbing Belarus and embarking on a series of costly (and unresolved) military conflicts with Ukraine and other countries on its immediate periphery.

In Washington, officials have begun to raise a number of grim questions: Could *jihadist* forces seize control of Russia's nuclear weapons? Might Russia try to buy off Islamists by selling nuclear weapons to Muslim countries? How should the United States and other Western powers react if Moscow overtly threatens Eastern Europe and the Caucasus? If Russia and China go to war in the Far East, should the United States intervene? And if Russia collapses into internal chaos, will Washington be forced to come to its rescue, economically or militarily, or both?

The year 2040 is only some twenty-five years away, and while the scenarios outlined above are by no means inevitable, they are, as we will see, quite plausible.

THE BEAR IS BACK ... FOR NOW

For the moment, the unraveling of Russia is still far from the minds of most observers. In fact, Russia's future looks comparatively bright. While the decade that followed the Soviet Union's collapse in 1991 saw a Russia that was humbled and diminished, over the past dozen years it has roared back onto the international stage under the guidance of its current president, Vladimir Putin.

In the Middle East, Moscow has reverted to familiar Soviet-style balance-of-power politics. It has played a key role in propping up the regime of Bashar al-Assad in Damascus, prolonging the brutal war that is being waged by Syria's dictator against his own people.[1] Russia likewise remains an enabler of Iran's nuclear ambitions, providing political cover and crucial know-how to the Islamic Republic's atomic effort despite deepening international concerns.[2]

Moscow has similarly divided and conquered in Europe. Its brief but decisive 2008 war with neighboring Georgia succeeded in halting the eastward expansion of the North Atlantic Treaty Organization (NATO), a key post–Cold War goal of both Europe and the United States. More than a few European countries, meanwhile, have become the targets of Russian economic blackmail, with the Kremlin using its energy wealth to shape politics there.[3]

In its "near abroad" of Central Asia and the Caucasus, Moscow has managed to regain a lot of its lost stature. Over the past decade, it has reconstituted much of its former influence through the construction of new political blocs, such as the Collective Security Treaty Organization and Shanghai Cooperation Organization, and by manipulating the region's fragile regimes. At the same time, it has worked diligently to shoulder the United States out of important post–September 11 military basing arrangements and reemerge as the unquestioned power in the post-Soviet space.[4]

Russia's return to global prominence has been engineered by Vladimir Putin, who, since his ascent to power in the last days of 1999, has taken Russia in a dramatically different direction from his predecessor, Boris Yeltsin.

During the Yeltsin era, Russia had become known as the "wild east," a place where gangster capitalism ran amok,[5] organized crime was ubiquitous,[6] and worries abounded over the security of the country's vast nuclear arsenal.[7] But it also saw the rise of real pluralism and open political debate.

Putin, by contrast, has exploited weariness with economic instability to concentrate power in a repressive, centralized state. Putin's authoritarian regime rules by political fiat, rewards loyalists through a vast network of corruption, and cows its political opponents into silence.[8] It simultaneously maintains its popularity through nationalistic posturing. Two decades after the Soviet collapse, Russia is ruled by a government that is consumed with its own financial well-being and global status but neglectful of the long-term needs of its people.

Not surprisingly, military modernization has become a central plank of Putin's agenda. Over the past decade, the Russian government has made major investments in its strategic forces with the aim of building a "twenty-first-century nuclear arsenal" that can overwhelm missile defenses and threaten the West.[9] This effort has included the creation of new intercontinental ballistic missiles, the deployment of additional long-range strike capabilities, and serious work on electromagnetic pulse weapons, with an additional estimated $600 billion to be spent on improving Russia's military capabilities through the end of the decade.[10]

Russia has done this even as the United States has sought to reduce its own capabilities. Since coming to power, the Obama administration has consistently advocated the total elimination of nuclear weapons, a concept colloquially known as "global zero," and made significant reductions to America's strategic arsenal in pursuit of that objective. President Obama's second term will include still more such cuts.[11]

The goal of Putin's policies is to reclaim Russia's geopolitical greatness. In 2005, in his annual state of the nation address to the Russian parliament, Putin referred to the collapse of the Soviet Union as the "greatest geopolitical catastrophe" of the last century.[12] Putin's comments created a firestorm in the West, where memories of the "Evil Empire" are still fresh. But at home, his words resonated with many Russians. It's easy to see why; an October 2012 survey conducted by the Carnegie Endowment for International Peace found that a third of Russians polled approved of or admired former Soviet dictator Joseph Stalin, while an equal number said that Russia needs a strong ruler like him. Support for Stalin had actually *increased* since the end of the Soviet Union. Surveying these discouraging results, Russia expert Masha Lipmann concluded that the "Russian people still have not come to terms with Stalin's legacy."[13]

Nor have they abandoned the idea of their country's destiny as a great power. This concept, known as *derzhavnost*, has animated Russian politics for centuries, driving successive czars to wage wars of conquest to expand the territories under their rule. Today, Putin's government has harnessed *derzhavnost* in its efforts to create a neo-Soviet sphere—a post-modern empire of extended Kremlin influence (if not actual territorial control).[14]

Russia likewise has demonstrated a growing willingness to challenge America strategically. Even as policymakers in Washington have sought to "reset" political relations with Moscow, the Russian government has revived a corrosive brand of anti-Americanism that views the United States as Russia's "main enemy" and geopolitical rival. Russia's more aggressive stance toward the United States was evident in 2012 when it twice violated the territorial sovereignty of the United States by carrying out aerial maneuvers inside the U.S. air defense zone. The moves were shockingly reminiscent of Soviet provocations during the Cold War.[15]

THE REAL THREAT FROM RUSSIA

In crafting their policies, Western governments have taken for granted that Russia, once weak, is now resurgent and that Moscow must be accommodated, or at least engaged.

Yet, for all of the Kremlin's current geopolitical posturing, Russia's revival will be fleeting, because the Russian Federation is fast approaching a massive social and political upheaval that promises to be as transformative as the USSR's demise some two decades ago. Russia's coming crisis is driven by the convergence of three trends:

Russia is dying. Russia is undergoing a catastrophic post-Soviet societal decline due to abysmal health standards, runaway drug addiction, and an AIDS crisis that officials have termed an "epidemic." The population of the Russian Federation is declining by close to half a million souls every year due to death and emigration.

At this rate, the once-mighty Russian state could lose a quarter of its population by the middle of this century. And according to some projections, if Russia's demographic trajectory does not change, its population could plummet to as little as fifty-two million people by 2080.[16] It's a phenomenon demographers have described as "the emptying of Russia"—a wholesale implosion of Russia's human capital and a collapse of its prospects as a viable modern state.[17]

Russia is transforming. Russia is experiencing a radical change in its ethnic and religious composition. Today, Russia's estimated twenty-one million Muslims are still a distinct minority. But Muslims are on track to account for a fifth of the country's population by the end of this decade, and a majority by mid-century.[18] Such a demographic revolution will fundamentally change Russia's character. That is not a problem, per se. But in recent years, the Kremlin has discriminated against its Muslim minority and ignored (even abetted) the rise of xenophobia among its citizens. This has bred resentment and alienation among Russia's Muslims, sentiments that radical Islamic groups have begun to exploit. The result is an increasingly restive Muslim minority with little connection to—or love for—the Russian state.

The Chinese are coming. A decline in Russia's population east of the Ural Mountains and a loosening of Kremlin control over the country's resource-rich east has sharpened the strategic competition with neighboring China and brought long-buried tensions over the future of the region back to the surface. In this unfolding conflict, China, a rising global economic and strategic power, holds the upper hand over a declining Russia. And, because it does, China could soon grow bold enough to challenge Russia for dominion over the latter's economically vital eastern territories.

WHY RUSSIAN WEAKNESS MATTERS

This perfect storm of demographic change, religious transformation, and external pressure will determine Russia's internal political climate, its place in the world, and its future strategic priorities.

Russia's revival will cause short-term tactical problems for the United States and its allies in the West. But further into the future, the strategic challenge posed by Russia will be even more profound. If the twentieth century was defined in large part by the rise of Russia (in the form of the Soviet Union), the twenty-first will be shaped in great measure by its unraveling.

This book is about that decline and its logical end product: the end of Russia itself. To be sure, the Russian Federation might not cease to exist altogether. In fact, it may yet linger on for some time to come. But the economic and social indicators are unmistakable: the Russia of tomorrow will look radically different from that of today. And when it does happen, Russia's implosion will threaten the United States and American interests in new and grave ways.

Policymakers in Washington would be wise not only to understand this reality, but also to begin planning for it.

CHAPTER TWO

THE NEW SICK MAN OF EUROPE

A century ago, the Ottoman Empire was known as the "sick man of Europe." At the height of its power in the seventeenth century, its territory and influence stretched from Africa to Asia and encompassed thirty-nine million people in more than thirty nations—nearly a tenth of the world's population at the time. But by the early twentieth century, Ottoman rule was in terminal decline, riven by conflicts along its periphery and torn apart by internal political strife. Its death throes contributed to the outbreak of the First World War and helped redraw the geopolitical map of the West.

Today, Russia has assumed the mantle of Europe's "sick man." The causes of Russia's illness include low birth rates, meager life expectancy, a culture of abortion, the collapse of the Russian family, and an escalating AIDS epidemic. The results are nothing short of catastrophic; at its current rate of decline, the population of the Russian Federation could plummet to just over one hundred million souls by the middle of this century.[1]

RUSSIA'S DEPOPULATION BOMB

Demography, it is often said, is destiny. How a population changes over time can determine whether a nation succeeds or fails. Yet few students of international affairs pay much attention to demographics, preferring to focus on subjects such as military history and strategic culture. Fewer still appreciate the profound impact that demography has on the course of global geopolitics.

So it is with Russia. For years, a handful of scholars have sounded the alarm over Russia's unfolding demographic disaster and its dire strategic implications for Russia and the West. In the main, however, Russia's demographic collapse is still poorly understood and underappreciated among both policymakers in Washington and the American public at large.

The math behind Russia's decline is complex, and stark. Countries require an average of 2.1 live births per woman to maintain a stable population. That formula is known as the "total fertility rate," or TFR. Today, the countries of Africa have the highest TFRs in the world, ranging from the prolific (Niger: 7.61) to the merely robust (Zimbabwe: 3.61).[2] In other words, in much of Africa societal continuity is not in question (even though a host of other issues—from economic prosperity to political stability—are).

Other countries, such as Turkey, Nicaragua, and Turkmenistan, generally have stable populations, with fertility at right around the rate necessary for replenishment.[3] The United States is among them: America's TFR is more or less stable at 2.06, thanks in part to high levels of immigration (mostly from Latin American countries).

Other countries are dying, with fertility rates far below replacement levels. Canada's is 1.59; Japan's just 1.39.[4] The TFRs of most European countries are lower still, with a median of just 1.38. This has led columnist Mark Steyn to wryly observe that, "Unless it corrects course within the next five to ten years, Europe by the end of this century will be a continent after the neutron bomb: the grand buildings will be standing but the people who built them will be gone."[5]

In this grim calculus, Russia ranks close to the bottom. According to U.S. Census Bureau statistics, in the years between 2000 and 2008, Russia's average annual fertility rate was 1.34, far below the 2.1 necessary to maintain a population at its current size.[6]

Today, the situation is a bit better. According to U.S. government estimates, Russia now ranks 178th in the world, with a TFR of 1.61.[7] And in 2012, for the first time since the fall of the USSR, live births outnumbered deaths in Russia. They did so modestly (the country's population grew by just over two hundred thousand between January and September 2012), but it was enough for Kremlin officials to proclaim that their country's demographic fortunes had been reversed.[8]

Experts are less optimistic. Some have cautioned that Russia's demographic reversal is fragile and temporary. In 2010, one of Russia's leading demographers, Anatoly Vishnevsky of the Moscow

Institute of Demography, warned, "In five years, Russia will again begin dying out." Vishnevsky noted that the "youth bulge" (and corresponding spike in fertility), which had slowed Russia's demographic decline, was close to being exhausted, and that as a result "the country is approaching the edge of a demographic abyss."[9] Recent studies have come to the same conclusion. A 2012 survey by Aton, a Moscow-based investment bank, concluded that Russia's current demographic upswing is only temporary and that the country "will soon face another protracted demographic decline."[10]

In truth, Russia's demographic descent is not a new or surprising phenomenon. Early signs of a population downturn began to appear as long ago as the 1960s, and by the 1970s total fertility had dropped to less than two children per woman in almost all of the Soviet Union's European republics.[11]

But these facts did not comport with the Soviet Union's view of itself as a great and growing power. Thus in early 1991, just months before the USSR's collapse, the Institute for Scientific Information, a research center of the prestigious Soviet Academy of Sciences, issued a rosy outlook on Soviet demography. Internal population growth within the Soviet Union was strong, the study declared, and the number of ethnic Russians within the USSR would grow by as much as two million over the following half decade. By 2015, the report predicted, ethnic Russians would number 158 million.[12]

The reality has proven to be very different. Russia's most recent national census found that the population of Russia shrank by nearly 3 percent in the eight years between 2002 and 2010 and now stands at 142.9 million.[13] If current trends continue, by 2050 official Kremlin estimates project that Russia's population will dwindle to just 107 million.[14]

THE DRIVERS OF DECLINE

Russia's demographic decline is a consequence of societal dysfunctions that took root during the decades of repressive Communist rule. Here is a brief description of just a few of those drivers.

SKY-HIGH MORTALITY

The years that followed the breakup of the USSR were economically and politically tumultuous for the countries of the former Soviet Union. The human cost of Russia's transition was particularly severe, with many post-Soviet countries seeing dramatic drops in life expectancy.

During the Cold War, life expectancy in Russia was only slightly lower than in the United States. But as the decades of political and military tension between Moscow and Washington wore on, a real—and widening—mortality gap emerged. The gap narrowed in the 1980s with Mikhail Gorbachev's policy of *perestroika* (and its attendant focus on public health). But following the Soviet collapse, Russian life expectancy again plummeted, dropping some 6.6 years for men and 3.3 years for women between 1989 and 1994.[15]

While the mortality rates of most other countries affected by the USSR's crack-up have largely stabilized, Russian life expectancy has remained low. In 2004, Russia ranked 122nd in the world in life expectancy, placing it in the bottom third of all nations and far outside the norm for industrialized ones.[16] By 2011, that number had plunged some twenty-two places, to 144th.[17] The average life expectancy for Russian citizens is now seventy years, putting them behind the citizens of Peru and Tonga (average life expectancy: seventy-one) and only slightly ahead of those in countries such as Tuvalu, Mongolia, and North Korea.[18]

Russian males have been particularly hard-hit. On average, they can expect to live just sixty years—less than their counterparts born in Botswana, Madagascar, and Yemen. The life expectancy of Russian males is, generally, a decade and a half shorter than those in other industrialized nations.[19]

The situation for Russian women is slightly better. Females there can expect to live until they are seventy-three, roughly the same age as women in neighboring Kazakhstan or in Saudi Arabia and Indonesia.[20] But, like Russian men, Russian women have nothing resembling the life expectancy of their counterparts in the West.

Russia's plummeting life expectancy is counterintuitive. "The Russian experience grates against conventional wisdom about the progress of global health and social standards over the last century," Nicholas Eberstadt and Apoorva Shah of the American Enterprise Institute have written. "It is unprecedented for a well-educated, modern European society to mimic mortality rates of a Third World country."[21] And yet, that is exactly what Russia has done.

The causes are many, from poor healthcare to rampant alcoholism, particularly among Russian men. Russian scientists estimate that one in five male deaths in Russia today is alcohol-related.[22] And while alcoholism is a problem across Russian society, the country's youth are disproportionately affected. Alcoholism among Russian youth contributes to a death rate at age thirty-five that is seven times that found in the European Union, according to Yuri Krupnov, director of Moscow's Institute of Demography, Migration and Regional Development.[23]

Russia's drinking problem may be contributing to its decline, but it's not the only factor. Russia is coming apart at a more fundamental level.

COLLAPSE OF THE RUSSIAN FAMILY

During the early part of the Cold War, the harsh realities of life under Communist rule kept families unified and tightly knit. Communal apartments, colloquially known as *komunalki*, were typical, as was having multiple generations of one family living under the same roof. In 1958, divorces in the USSR were virtually nonexistent— just 0.9 per one thousand citizens.[24] By the end of the 1970s, that rate had risen slightly to 3.6 per one thousand.[25] But Soviet-era restrictions on individual mobility, coupled with widespread economic hardship, helped keep most families together.

By contrast, the past two decades of freewheeling capitalism and post-Communist disorder have coincided with a collapse of the Russian family. According to the UN's 2011 *Demographic Yearbook*, Russia now has the highest divorce rate in the world, with half of all unions ending in divorce (and 60 percent of those dissolving within the first decade).[26]

This does not mean that Russians are not procreating. Far from it, as the abortion rate (discussed below) indicates. It suggests, rather, that nuclear families with multiple children are quickly becoming an endangered species in Russia.

A CULTURE OF ABORTION

Under Communist rule, abortion was the only practical method of birth control available to Soviet citizens, and it was employed extensively. In 1964, there were 278 abortions for every one hundred live births in the USSR, a rate that far outpaced those in the West.[27] Russia's abortion rate remained high through the 1970s and 1980s, with the number of abortions exceeding 4.5 million annually.[28]

Russia's abortion rate gradually began to decline as Soviet authorities—and then Russian ones—became more conscious of the negative effects of abortion, and more restrictive in its authorization. In 2006, for the first time, the trend reversed, with ninety-five abortions for every hundred live births.[29]

But this progress is relative. Russia still has the highest abortion rate in the world. In 2010, 1,186,000 abortions were performed in Russia—that's three hundred abortions every hour.[30] It also means that close to one percent of the country's population is being aborted every year—literally killing chances for positive population growth in the process.

But the official estimates may not capture the true extent of Russia's abortion culture. According to Igor Beloborodov of Moscow's Institute of Demographic Studies, the actual number of annual abortions performed in Russia is as much as double the official figure—some 2 to 2.5 million in all—owing to "a vast layer of private clinics" that carry out the procedure in parallel to official hospitals and facilities.[31] If Beloborodov's tally is accurate, then the true cost of Russia's abortion culture is the annual termination of close to 2 percent of the Russian Federation's potential population. In a real sense, Russians are aborting their future.

AN AIDS EPIDEMIC

HIV/AIDS first appeared in Russia later than it did in other parts of the world, in part because of a lack of mobility and travel among the captive population of the Soviet Union during the Cold War. Russia registered its first cases of HIV/AIDS in 1987—half a decade after the disease became prevalent in the West.[32]

Once AIDS did arrive in post-Soviet Russia, however, it spread quickly. By the end of the 1990s, documented cases of AIDS in the Russian Federation stood at approximately twenty thousand. Less than a decade later, Russian experts began calling their country's encounter with HIV an epidemic. "We have an estimate of up to 1.2 million to 1.3 million infected with HIV," Vadim Pokrovsky, head of the Russian government's AIDS center, told reporters in May 2007.[33] "Not only is the number of Russians infected with HIV rising but there is an increase in the rate at which the epidemic is spreading, so [there is] a rise in the number of newly infected."[34]

Blood infected by HIV, the virus that causes AIDS, spreads easily when people share equipment to use drugs. Some 2.5 million Russians are estimated to be addicted to drugs today, with heroin as the overwhelming drug of choice.[35] According to the UN Office of Drugs and Crime, Russian consumption accounts for more than a fifth of all heroin consumed globally every year. This trend has contributed greatly to the spread of AIDS in Russia. According to a 2012 briefing paper compiled by the International AIDS Society, more than one third of the country's users of injectable drugs have HIV.[36]

Over the past decade, AIDS-related deaths in Eastern Europe and Central Asia have skyrocketed, increasing elevenfold since 2001. Russia and Ukraine cumulatively accounted for roughly 90 percent of the ninety thousand AIDS deaths in the region in 2010.[37] That statistic stands out even more when compared with the rest of the world, where AIDS deaths have fallen by more than a fifth since their peak in 2005.[38] In other words, while the rest of the world is beginning to win the battle against AIDS, the Russian Federation is increasingly succumbing to it.

A FLEEING POPULATION

Russians have been fleeing their homeland for decades. During the decades of the Cold War, Soviet rule was punctuated by repeated waves of politically and religiously motivated flight. Even so, the pace at which people are leaving Russia today is notable—and deeply concerning. Between 100,000 and 150,000 Russians now emigrate every year, compounding Russia's population crisis.[39]

Russians are fleeing for both economic and political reasons. A 2011 poll by the Moscow-based Levada Center identified economic pressures—such as the high cost of living—as principal factors in Russians' decision to depart.[40] But much of the blame rests with the Russian government as well. Over the past decade, the autocratic state established by Vladimir Putin and his followers has made a tiny minority of Russians wildly rich, while the vast majority of Russians are left to grapple with an environment that is deeply toxic to entrepreneurship, innovation, and honest business. This includes high-profile instances of Kremlin retribution against those who seek to change the status quo. One such victim was lawyer Sergei Magnitsky, who was imprisoned in 2009 for his investigation into official government corruption, and who subsequently died behind bars after being denied medical treatment for gallstones and pancreatitis.

The result is an exodus of Russians that rivals in size and scope the mass out-migration that followed the 1917 Bolshevik Revolution. "The most independent and qualified people are leaving and for the same fundamental reasons," political scientist Dmitry Oreshkin noted in the newspaper *Novaya Gazeta* in January 2011. "The model of the state built by Lenin and Stalin and softly being restored by Putin is flawed from the outset."[41]

More than two million people are believed to have left Russia during the thirteen years that President Vladimir Putin has been in power.[42] Many of those who stay are thinking of leaving. A 2012 poll by the RIA Novosti news agency found that one in five Russians desires to live abroad.[43] The problem is particularly acute among Russia's youth: according to one estimate, nearly 40 percent of Russians between the ages of eighteen and thirty-five are contemplating departure.[44]

This mass exodus is having a devastating effect on the Russian economy. By 2030, it is estimated that the country will lose as many as seventeen million skilled workers—close to a quarter of its total workforce of 75.4 million.[45] Farther into the future, Russia's working population is projected to be smaller still, with catastrophic effects on the country's productivity and economic dynamism. (So profound has this trend become that the International Monetary Fund recently suggested that the Russian government raise the retirement age to sixty-three by 2030 in order to preserve its labor force.)[46]

REMEDYING THE PROBLEM?

Russians are not ignorant of their demographic dilemma, and neither is the Kremlin. Putin has described Russia's demographic decline as "the most acute problem of contemporary Russia."[47] But his government has not implemented a plausible strategy for remedying the situation. Rather, preoccupied with regaining its place as a global power, it has only peripherally begun to address the drivers of national decline.

In 2008, for example, Russia established a Day of Married Love and Family Happiness—portrayed as an alternative to Valentine's Day—in an effort to reinforce the importance of the family unit.[48] In 2010, the Russian government launched the "mother's capital" program, which provides a government credit of about $11,000 to mothers who have a second or third child.[49] This was followed by the announcement in April 2011 that the Russian government would invest some 1.5 trillion rubles ($50 billion) into "demography projects."[50] The same month, the Duma, Russia's lower house of parliament, introduced legislation to discourage abortion by disqualifying it from coverage under the national medical service. That summer, then president Dmitry Medvedev signed the first law since the end of communism to restrict abortion.[51]

More recently, Putin pledged that families with more than three children will receive monthly subsidies of $250 per child.[52] The Kremlin has become so desperate to encourage procreation that in early 2013 it tried to turn 1990s R&B crooners Boyz II Men into demographic Viagra. The group was invited to Moscow to play a Valentine's Day concert in hopes that their music would make concertgoers amorous, leading to lovemaking.[53]

What Russia has *not* done is make serious investments in vital infrastructure—the social services and education that cumulatively serve as the lifeblood of a vibrant society. Unlike the United States, which used the 1990s to rebuild and reorient its economy toward domestic prosperity, Russia experienced no analogous "peace dividend" following the collapse of the USSR. Rather, Russia limped through its first post-Soviet decade buffeted by economic instability, culminating in a catastrophic economic meltdown in 1998.

In the last dozen years, Russia's economy has stabilized, largely due to the high price of world energy and Russia's emergence as a bona fide oil and natural gas powerhouse. But Russia's energy boom has not translated into meaningful improvements to the country's social safety net. According to a 2011 study by the European Union, Russia's healthcare expenditures have stagnated as a percentage of GDP since 1995.[54] Nor are there many plans for upgrades on the horizon. In September 2012, Deputy Economic Development Minister Andrey Klepach announced that no reform in the education, public health, and science sectors was possible in the near term because of the government's budget priorities.[55]

What are those priorities, exactly? Over the past decade, Russia's national treasure has been expended overwhelmingly on projects that reaffirm its image and perception of itself as a great power. These include the country's strategic arsenal, which is now undergoing a major modernization aimed in part at countering and defeating U.S. missile defenses.[56] But the quiet human catastrophe now reshaping Russia at home has been left largely unaddressed.

A CRISIS OF CONFIDENCE

What makes Russia's demographic decline so devastating is that it reflects the outlook many Russians have of themselves. The trends—high mortality, rampant alcoholism and drug use, widespread abortion and divorce, and emigration—are the symptoms of a population that has lost hope in its future, and of a citizenry that has given up on their government as a steward of their needs and protector of their rights and freedoms.

The results have been predictable. Russians with the means to leave have already done so or are actively contemplating an exit. (In an accurate microcosm of the prevailing mood among Russians, a popular blog on current social ills is entitled *Pora Valit*: time to scram.)[57] Those who are unable to leave have embraced alcohol, drugs, and other means of coping to get by. And still others have gone to even greater extremes: in the two decades following the collapse of the Soviet Union, an estimated eight hundred thousand Russians have committed suicide.[58] That is one suicide every fifteen minutes.

In a nation that is coming apart, many of Russia's citizens appear to be united by one thing: the stark realization that, for all of the Kremlin's talk of renewed national greatness, the Russian state is a dying project.

CHAPTER THREE

MUSLIM RUSSIA RISING

In the late summer of 2005, Russia's most prominent Muslim weighed in on the national debate taking place over the country's dismal demographics. In an address to the European Union of Muslims, Ravil Gaynutdin, Russia's chief mufti, said, "The number of people professing Islam in Russia is constantly growing." In fact, according to Gaynutdin, there were as many as twenty-three million Russian Muslims—nearly ten million more than the 14.5 million officially tallied by the country's census that year.[1]

Predictably, Gaynutdin's comments touched off a firestorm of controversy, with detractors insisting that the cleric's figures were grossly inflated. Perhaps they were: Russia's 2002 census had contained a much more modest official estimate, pegging the number of Muslims at approximately fifteen million, or 10 percent of the population.[2] Notably, though, the Russian Orthodox Church—which has a vested interest in tracking the number of Muslims in Russia—had given its own estimate not long prior. At twenty million, it was much closer to Gaynutdin's projections than to those of the Kremlin.[3]

Regardless of which estimate is correct, the incident cast light on how quickly Islam has gained ground in Russia. While Russia's Slavic population is constricting, Russia's Muslims are faring a good deal better. In fact, Islam can be said to be experiencing a major—and sustained—revival there.

A POST-SOVIET RENAISSANCE

While Muslims have lived on what is now Russian territory for centuries (mostly concentrated in the Volga and North Caucasus regions), the rise of what can be called "Muslim Russia" has taken place mostly during the post-Soviet era.

At the end of the Cold War in 1989, Muslims made up 19.2 percent of the overall Soviet population of nearly 287 million.[4] But the Soviet Union was formally atheist, which meant that Islam, like all other organized religions, was closely regulated and tightly controlled by the state. (Mass deportations and forcible relocations of Chechen, Ingush, and Crimean Muslims during Stalin's reign contributed to the overall repression.)[5]

With the breakup of the USSR, the number of Muslims in Russia initially fell sharply—only around ten million remained in post-Soviet Russia (accounting for 7 percent of the country's then-148-million-person population).[6] But relatively robust birth rates since then have swelled the ranks of Russia's Muslims relative to their Slavic counterparts.

According to Russia's 2002 census, the country's overall Muslim population grew by 20 percent between 1989 and 2002.[7] During the same period, the country's Slavic population declined by nearly 4 percent.[8] And this trajectory is continuing—United Nations estimates put Russia's overall fertility rate at much lower than Russian Muslims' fertility rate of 2.3.[9] Other estimates have placed the fertility rate among Russia's Muslims at higher still: between six and ten children per woman, depending on where in the Russian Federation they live.[10] Whatever the actual number, it is clear—as a 2005 study commissioned by the Washington, D.C.–based Center for Strategic and International Studies put it—that "Russia's Muslims ... have significantly more babies, suffer less premature death, and live longer than do Russia's Slavs."[11]

The disparity is easy to explain. Studies have found that Muslim women in Russia are more likely to marry, less likely to divorce, and less likely to have abortions than non-Muslim women in Russia.[12] Between 1991 and 2011, the number of Russian Muslims nearly tripled, and now rests at a median estimate of about twenty-one million—or roughly 15 percent of the country's total population.[13]

80 percent of Russia's Muslims reside in the North Caucasus and Middle Volga regions.[14] In the republic of Chechnya (in the North Caucasus), the population is expected to grow 47 percent, from 1.2 million to 1.8 million, by 2030.[15] The neighboring North Caucasus

republics of Dagestan and Ingushetia are also predicted to grow rapidly in the years ahead.[16] Most of the rest of Russia, by contrast, will not.

Russia's indigenous Muslim population has been bolstered by an influx of three to four million Muslim migrants from former Soviet states such as Azerbaijan and Kazakhstan who have entered Russia in search of employment.[17]

As the number of Russian Muslims has grown, so has their public presence. In 1991, there were hundreds of mosques in Russia. Today there are at least eight thousand, with much of the new construction being paid for by funds from the Middle East.[18] Similarly, in 1991 just forty-one Russians made the *hajj* pilgrimage to Mecca, Saudi Arabia—a religious duty that must be carried out by every able-bodied Muslim who can afford to do so at least once in his or her lifetime. In 2009, an estimated forty thousand did.[19] And Moscow, Russia's capital, is now home to an estimated 2.5 million Muslims—more than any other European city except for Istanbul, Turkey.[20]

The implications of Islam's ascendance in Russia are hard to overstate. "Russia is going through a religious transformation that will be of even greater consequence for the international community than the collapse of the Soviet Union," Paul Goble, a leading expert on Russia's Muslims, has said.[21]

Russia's religious transformation is still unfolding. At their current rate of growth, Muslims will make up one-fifth of Russia's population by 2020.[22] And by the middle of this century, officials in Moscow predict that the Russian Federation might become majority Muslim.[23]

But the effects of this change could be felt much sooner. "[T]he growing number of people of Muslim background in Russia will have a profound impact on Russian foreign policy," Goble maintains. "The assumption in Western Europe or the United States that Moscow is part of the European concert of powers is no longer valid."[24]

LEFT BEHIND

Islam's revival in Russia would be seen as a neutral—perhaps even a beneficial—development if Muslims were fully integrated into Russian culture and society. But they are not. Indeed, by most socioeconomic measures, Muslims are faring much more poorly than other Russians. As scholar Gordon Hahn has noted, "Russia's poorest regions are most often those heavily populated with Muslims."[25]

The disparities are most striking in the Muslim-dominated republics of the North Caucasus. In 2011, more than half of the population of Ingushetia was jobless, as was 42 percent of Russians in Chechnya and Dagestan, and 17 percent living in Kabardino-Balkaria.[26] (By way of comparison, the national unemployment rate in Russia in 2011 was approximately 7 percent.)[27] So, while the North Caucasus "is only home to one in fifteen inhabitants of the Russian Federation," a 2011 study on Russian demographics by the Berlin Institute for Population and Development pointed out, "it is home to one in seven of the unemployed."[28]

Crippling poverty is also pervasive among the areas of Russia dominated by Muslims. In 2005, the Russian government estimated that more than 90 percent of Chechnya's population was living below the poverty line, earning less than seventy-two euros (approx-imately $100) a month.[29] Today, the situation is only marginally better. Despite years of aid disbursements from Moscow and finan-cial contributions from concerned countries in Europe, Chechnya's poverty rate still stands at 80 percent.[30] Ingushetia, Dagestan, and Kabardino-Balkaria post similarly bleak statistics—a symptom of a prosperity gap between the North Caucasus and the rest of Russia that is widening despite improvements to the country's overall economy.

The economic crisis in the North Caucasus has produced a flour-ishing black market and underground economy there. By some estimates, 70 percent of the financial activity in Dagestan is generated in the region's shadow economy.[31] And it is not alone. According to official statistics, nearly a third of all economic activity in Russia's Southern District—which encompasses Dagestan, Chechnya, and Ingushetia, as well as the republics of Adygeya, Kabardino-Balkaria, North Ossetia, and Karachaevo-Cherkessia—derives from illicit trade and informal financial transfers.[32]

The Muslim regions of Russia's heartland have fared better—thanks largely to the area's role as a hub for energy and trade. As of 2010, unemployment rates in the republics of Tatarstan and Bash-kortostan were officially estimated at 7.7 and 9.6, respectively—roughly equal to the national average.[33] Nevertheless, problems remain. According to the United Nations Development Programme, in 2005, the Middle Volga region's overall poverty rate was between 22 and 30 percent.[34]

These statistics are telling. A pronounced prosperity gap has emerged between Russia's Muslim and Slavic populations. "Muslims are more likely to be unemployed, to have a wage below the subsistence minimum, and to have below-average-sized apartments," a recent study dissecting statistics from Russia's 2002 Census concluded.[35] The result is an expanding Muslim underclass that is seen, and that sees itself, as separate from the rest of Russia.

A BACKLASH FROM BELOW

On December 11, 2010, Moscow's famed Manezh Square, just steps from the Kremlin, was overrun by demonstrators from Russia's Far Right. The occasion was a rally of some five thousand soccer fans and nationalists memorializing Yegor Sviridov, a backer of Russia's Spartak soccer club who had died a week earlier in a clash with other fans, many of them migrants from the Caucasus. The rally quickly deteriorated into a race riot, and thirty people—most of them immigrants—were injured in the violence, some at the hands of the Kremlin's security forces.

The Manezh riot was far from an isolated event. Recent years have seen a marked increase in xenophobia, racism, and violence against non-Slavs within the Russian Federation. Experts say they are a reflection of widespread anger over economic stagnation and corruption. They are also a reaction to a surge of migrant workers from Russia's "near abroad" of the Caucasus and Central Asia. With foreign arrivals now totaling thirteen to fourteen million, Russia's migrant labor force ranks second only to the United States.[36]

But whereas the United States largely assimilates its immigrants, Russia does not. According to research conducted by Mark Ustinov of Moscow's Higher School of Economics, nearly 70 percent of Russians exhibit negative feelings toward people of other ethnicities, and one in five believes that they have no place in Russia.[37] Most Russians, moreover, want their government to do something about it. A November 2012 nationwide opinion poll carried out by Moscow's Levada Analytical Center found that nearly 65 percent of respondents favor some form of restrictions on labor migration.[38]

Not surprisingly, race-related violence in Russia has surged in recent years, especially in Moscow and other cities. In 2012 alone, eighteen people were killed and nearly two hundred were injured in racist attacks throughout Russia, according to estimates by SOVA, a Russian human rights watchdog group.[39] But experts say the real number is probably much higher, since most attacks go unreported.[40]

The rise in ethnic violence in Russia has been propelled by a surge in extreme right-wing nationalism. Historically, nationalist ideas and rhetoric have pervaded Russian politics, empowering *derzhavnost*—the idea of Russia as a great power—and helping to define a sense of self among the country's citizens during turbulent economic and political times. But today's Far Right in Russia goes far beyond the nationalist rhetoric espoused by parties like Vladimir Zhirinovsky's Liberal-Democratic Party of Russia (LDPR) and Dmitry Rogozin's now-defunct *Rodina* (Motherland) faction. It is made up of an assortment of small, violent neo-Nazi groups and "political nationalists," such as the *Russkiye* movement and the *Novaya Sila* party, that promote an ethno-nationalist agenda in Russian politics.[41] These right-wing groups are growing in influence. "Although the extreme right remains a marginal phenomenon in

Russian politics up to now," Alexander Verkhovsky of SOVA has written, "it is a widely held view in Russian society that nationalism is an ideology with a future and will gain more popularity in the years to come."[42]

The Far Right's ascendance has been aided by the Kremlin, which has sought to harness nationalist sentiment for its own ends.[43] While cracking down on the most violent offenders, Vladimir Putin's government has nurtured nationalist ideas via youth groups like *Nashi*, Walking Together, and the Young Guard—groups whose members tend to share a common vision with Russia's ultra-right.[44]

Russian nationalism is not only a Far Right notion, however. More and more, Russians from across the political spectrum are identifying with and organizing around a nationalism that is increasingly tinged with racism. "The level of xenophobia today is rising among various social groups," Russia's Civic Chamber, an official civil society oversight body created by Vladimir Putin in the early 2000s, noted in its 2012 annual report. "An especially sharp rise can be observed among the citizens of major cities and among those people with a high level of education. Their phobias relate first and foremost to migrants from the Caucasus and Central Asia, and are motivated by 'insurmountable' cultural differences."[45] The result has been the creation of what one specialist has called a "fashion for xenophobia" throughout the country.[46]

Resentment among ordinary Russians over ongoing violence in the Caucasus and protectionist sentiments toward jobs taken by migrant workers have heightened tensions and made Russia's Muslims an easy target.

ISOLATION FROM ABOVE

The Kremlin's actions haven't helped. Over the past dozen years, Putin's government has carried out what amounts to an "authoritarian counter-revolution" in Russia.[47]

During Boris Yeltsin's presidency in the 1990s, Russia's shattered economy and uncertain political direction helped to incubate deep internal divides within the Russian government.

Putin consequently made "strengthen[ing] the unity of the state" a central focus of his administration from the time he succeeded Yeltsin in 1999.[48] Putin's efforts resulted in a dramatic increase in central authority—what Kremlin insiders call the "power vertical." This centralization was accomplished by:

Taking power away from Russia's regions. Among the first steps taken by the Putin government was the creation of seven new federal "super districts" to oversee the country's eighty-eight (now eighty-three) regions. Each corresponded roughly with the country's military districts and was headed by a special representative appointed by the Kremlin. In addition, a change was made in governance in Russia's various regions and oblasts: governors and the presidents of the country's constituent republics would henceforth be appointed by presidential decree rather than by popular election.[49] That meant that Moscow, not the Russian electorate, now possessed the power to fire regional officials, who were no longer elected but selected—reversing a trend of the Yeltsin era that saw tentative steps toward democratization and federalism.

Turning Russia's parliament into a rubber-stamp body. Since Putin's assumption of power in 2000, his political party, United Russia, has become the unquestioned power broker in Russian politics, securing and maintaining controlling interest in Russia's lower house of parliament, the State Duma. Reforms initiated by the Putin government have fundamentally altered the character of the legislature's upper house, the Federation Council. Representatives are now appointed by the president (rather than elected by the people) and reflect his interests (rather than representing the people's).[50] At the same time, a 2004 law increased the barriers for political participation, raising the number of members a political party needs to legally register and thereby preserving United Russia's near-monopoly on power.[51]

Assuming greater oversight powers. The Kremlin passed the "Law on Combating Extremist Activity" in the aftermath of the September 2004 massacre carried out by Islamic extremists at a children's school in Beslan. The law granted the Kremlin the power to ban parties from elections if any of its members were found to be engaging in "extremist activities."[52] The Kremlin also enacted counter-terrorism laws that gave it greater police powers. And Putin signed into law new regulations requiring all non-governmental organizations to register with the government and comply with strict scrutiny over their activities. These measures were ostensibly meant to ensure that the organizations were meeting their objectives. But the implementation of these new policies followed a wave of "color revolutions" that had swept over the post-Soviet space (including Ukraine's 2004 Orange Revolution and Kyrgyzstan's 2005 Tulip Revolution). They were therefore interpreted as a not-so-subtle expression of the Kremlin's fears that Western-funded civil society groups would generate similar political upheaval in Russia.[53]

Putin's reforms were radical, but they coincided with sudden resource-based wealth generated by Russia's booming energy sector and a time of comparative political stability after the turbulent Yeltsin years. As a result, the public largely tolerated Putin's attempts to consolidate power.[54]

But Putin's reconfiguration shattered the fragile ethnic and social balance of power between Russia's regions and the so-called "federal center." Through centralization, the Kremlin left the country's minorities with no recourse—and no trust in the state. "[B]y dismantling federalism and democracy," Gordon Hahn noted in 2007, "Putin is destabilizing regional politics, providing an additional opening for ethno-nationalism, radical Islam and Islamist *jihadism* in Russia."[55]

A DANGEROUS DISTANCE

Hahn's observation turned out to be predictive. Not all of Russia's Muslims feel alienated and isolated, of course. But overall, the Kremlin's inattention to the country's Muslim minority and that community's difficult relationship with non-Muslim Russians have produced a deepening ideological distance between Russia's Muslims and the Russian state.[56]

According to Damir-Khazrat Mukhetdinov, deputy chairman of the Muslim Spiritual Directorate of European Russia, the Russian *umma* (community of believers) is "becoming increasingly polarized and atomized," and young Russian Muslims are demonstrating a "rejection of Russian society and of the Russian state."[57] This detachment, Mukhetdinov notes, has prompted many Russian

Muslims to embrace "ideological concepts that have come to us from abroad."[58]

Chief among these foreign ideological concepts is a virulent strain of radical Islam that, two decades after its introduction into the Russian Federation, now threatens the very integrity of the Russian state.

CHAPTER FOUR

RUSSIA'S HIDDEN WAR

In the morning of January 24, 2011, a twenty-year-old Muslim from the region of Ingushetia named Magomed Yevloyev hitched a ride to Domodedovo, Russia's busiest airport, located forty minutes south of Moscow. Yevloyev, a member of the Caucasus Emirate, Russia's most violent Islamist group, had arrived in the Russian capital several days earlier, where he met up with at least two accomplices. In Domodedovo, Yevloyev walked past the international terminal to the facility's luggage claim area, where he detonated a concealed explosive device containing shrapnel and as much as five pounds of TNT. The blast ripped through the bustling terminal, killing thirty-seven travelers and wounding nearly two hundred others.[1]

The suicide bombing, the second major terror incident to hit the Russian capital in less than a year, did more than murder and injure hundreds of people and temporarily bring air traffic in the Russian Federation to a standstill. It also exposed the dirty little secret the Kremlin has worked diligently to hide from the world. Some two decades into Russia's own version of the "war on terror," it is no longer possible to ignore the country's rising Islamist insurgency. Nor is it possible to ignore the fact that the Russian government, which once promised a swift, decisive victory over what it calls "Wahhabism," seems to have little idea what to do about it.

THE CHECHEN QUAGMIRE

It was not always this way. Two decades ago, the threat posed by Islamic radicalism was still distant to most Russians. True, the collapse of the USSR had unleashed a wave of ethnic separatism on the territory of the former Soviet Union. Over thirteen months, fifteen new countries, six of them majority-Muslim, emerged from the wreckage of the "Evil Empire." But the number of Muslims within Russia itself decreased as a result, and many of those who remained lacked a clear religious direction or sense of spiritual identity.

If the growth of Islamic radicalism was not an immediate concern, a further breakup of the Russian state was. The successful independence movements in the countries of the Caucasus and Central Asia ignited dreams of similar revolutions in many corners of the Russian Federation. This was particularly true in Russia's Caucasus republics—the majority-Muslim regions that abutted the newly independent nations of Georgia, Azerbaijan, and Armenia.

These stirrings culminated in the November 1991 declaration of independence by Chechnya's nationalist leader, Dzhokhar Dudayev.

Dudayev did not initially embrace Islam as the foundation for an independent Chechnya.[2] Slowly, however, the Chechen self-determination struggle transformed into an Islamist *jihad*. This was due in large part to an influx of "Afghan alumni"—foreign (mostly Arab) *mujahideen* who previously fought the Soviets in Afghanistan—into the breakaway republic in the early 1990s.[3] These forces helped bolster the ranks of the Chechen resistance against Russian troops, but they also served to progressively alter its character. Experts estimate that, soon after, some three hundred "Afghan" Arabs were active in Chechnya and engaged in hostilities there.[4] So was an array of other Islamist forces, from Saudi charities to al Qaeda, all of which had an interest in promoting a religious alternative to the Russian state.[5] By the time of the signing of the Khasavyurt agreement, which formally ended the First Chechen War in August 1996, Chechen politics had become both Islamized and internationalized—laying the groundwork for future conflict.

Instability followed, as the republic deteriorated into rampant criminality and lawlessness, often caused by local warlords such as Shamil Basayev, who strengthened the Chechen Islamist movement's ties to international terror and engaged in increasingly brazen acts of domestic terrorism.[6] This disorder, in turn, soon spread to neighboring Russian republics.[7]

Two events propelled Russia back into open conflict with its unruly hinterlands. The first was the August 1999 invasion of neighboring Dagestan by an Islamist militia led by Basayev and Jordanian-born *jihadi* commander Omar Ibn al Khattab. The second was the

September 1999 bombing of four apartment blocks in the Russian cities of Moscow, Buynansk, and Volgodonsk, allegedly by Chechen rebels. (Considerable controversy surrounds the terrorist attacks, with some claiming that the blasts were orchestrated by Russia's domestic intelligence service, the FSB, to provide a pretext for renewed war in the Caucasus.)[8]

But the nature of the conflict had changed fundamentally. The First Chechen War, at least in its opening stages, was mostly a struggle for self-determination. The war's second iteration had an overtly Islamist, missionary character. Instead of being localized to Chechnya, it increasingly implicated the republic's Caucasian neighbors (most directly Dagestan and Ingushetia). And while the First Chechen War took on the form of a fast-moving, asymmetric conflict, the second became a war of attrition, complete with a grinding, bloody ground campaign.

The Kremlin won a few victories in this effort. In April 2002, Russia's security services assassinated Khattab, the Jordanian-born *jihadist* rumored to be bin Laden's man in the Caucasus.[9] Four years later, in July 2006, warlord Shamil Basayev, the mastermind behind the 1999 Dagestan raid, was similarly dispatched.[10]

On the surface, these successes appeared to shift the momentum of the conflict in Moscow's favor, and the Kremlin was quick to declare victory. In April 2009, Prime Minister Vladimir Putin, in a Russian throwback to President George W. Bush's ill-considered May 2003 "mission accomplished" speech aboard the USS *Abraham Lincoln*, proudly declared victory in Russia's counterterrorism campaign.[11]

But that declaration of triumph turned out to be premature. By the end of 2009, extreme violence returned to the region. That year alone, the Caucasus Emirate carried out 511 terrorist attacks. By the end of the following year, the number had risen to 583.[12]

Today, despite regular public pronouncements to the contrary from officials in Moscow, whatever fleeting stability existed in the aftermath of the Russian military's onslaught has long since disappeared. The Caucasus remains a political quagmire for the Kremlin—and a locus of resilient Islamic radicalism. Indeed, over the past three years, Islamic militants in the region have staged a savage comeback, carrying out numerous atrocities, among them the brazen 2010 suicide raid on the Chechen parliament and the summer 2012 assassination of the spiritual leader of Dagestan's Sufi community.[13]

As violence has surged, Russian confidence has withered. A July 2010 exposé by Germany's influential news magazine *Der Spiegel* found that some high-ranking Russian officials have become convinced that it will take years to defeat extremist groups in the restive region—if such a feat can be accomplished at all.[14] Indeed, although the Russian government has vowed that the area will be safe for the 2014 Winter Olympics in nearby Sochi, local security has deteriorated to an unprecedented degree. Armored vehicles and helicopters are now *de rigueur* for all visiting Kremlin officials, and traffic policemen in the republic require the protection of Interior Ministry units. "It will take years to change the situation here," one Russian general told *Der Spiegel.* "For every dead terrorist, two new ones rise up to take his place."[15]

Islamism's resilience—indeed, its growing appeal—has a lot to do with a hardening of local attitudes. A poll conducted in early 2011 by the regional journal *Nations of Dagestan* found that 30 percent of Dagestani youth, including members of Dagestan's universities and police schools, said they would choose to live under a Muslim-run religious regime. More than a third of those polled indicated they would not turn in a friend or family member responsible for terrorism to authorities.[16] These findings mirror those of human rights groups and NGOs active in the Caucasus, which have documented an upsurge in support for Islamic extremism and adherence to radical religious ideas there.[17]

In other words, despite official claims that the region has been pacified, the North Caucasus is more and more a place where the Kremlin's authority is ignored, and even challenged, as well as where religious identity trumps nationalist sentiment. Worst of all, these problems are no longer isolated in Russia's periphery.

TROUBLE IN THE HEARTLAND

In Kazan, the capital of the Russian republic of Tatarstan, lies a bustling side street known as Gazovaya Ulitsa. There, you will find the Russian Islamic University, the region's premier Islamic school of higher learning. Founded in 1998, the university plays an important quasi-official role, promulgating the moderate Tatar version of Islam that is officially sanctioned by the Russian state. For its efforts, the university has been recognized by the Kremlin; the walls of its main hall are adorned with pictures of a 2009 official visit by then President Dmitry Medvedev.

But the Islamic University is not alone. Directly across the street sits the squat, imposing structure of the Eniler mosque. Built in the early 2000s thanks to funding from the Middle East, it has become one of the largest Wahhabi places of worship in the republic.[18]

The battle lines drawn along Gazovaya Ulitsa are emblematic of the ideological competition taking shape within Tatarstan—and across Russia's heartland as a whole. There, traditional, assimilationist Tatar Islam has increasingly found itself under siege from an insurgent and extreme Islamic fundamentalism.

To be sure, there are still many Muslims who follow the moderate Tatar interpretation of Islam. Of these, perhaps the most well known (albeit not the most mainstream) is Rafael Khakimov of the Tatarstan Academy of Sciences, who has written extensively about the idea of "Euro-Islam" and its compatibility with modernity.[19] Tatar Islam likewise remains the branch of the religion officially endorsed and embraced by the Russian state. But, as regional religious experts point out, the movement as a whole lacks a compelling overarching narrative that appeals to the region's Muslim youth.

Islamists, by contrast, do appeal to Russia's Muslim youth—a fact evident in the growth of Wahhabi grassroots activism in the form of social organizations, spiritual retreats, and informal youth gatherings, and in the growing number of local religious figures in the Volga region who espouse an extreme interpretation of Islam.

Russia's most virulent *jihadist* group, the Caucasus Emirate, does not yet appear to have much of an organized presence in the Volga region. But Doku Umarov, the group's leader, has talked publicly about the eventual expansion of *jihadist* activity along the Volga, and radical Islam's growth in Russia's heartland has become a topic of discussion among Russian Islamists.[20] Some early signs of militancy have emerged as a result. In February 2011, for example, security forces in the Bashkortostan region arrested four suspected Islamists from the western town of Oktyabrsky, including the purported leader of the local affiliate of Umarov's group.[21]

In addition, several small Tatar organizations—among them Ittifak, Milli Mejlis, and elements within the All-Tatar Public Center—have Islamist tendencies.[22] But the Islamist group with the most organized presence in Russia is the grassroots missionary organization known as Hizb-ut Tahrir (HuT). While formally eschewing religious violence, HuT pursues a phased agenda whose long-term goal is the creation of a caliphate and the imposition of Islamic law in the numerous countries and regions where it is active.[23] There is a strong correlation between membership in HuT and the eventual embrace of religiously motivated violence—so much so that experts have likened the group to a "conveyor belt of extremism."[24]

HuT has been formally banned in Russia since February 2003, when the country's Supreme Court designated it and fourteen other entities as terrorist groups. The Russian government has steadily persecuted the group since, launching a number of investigations into suspected criminal and terrorist activities by its members. Nevertheless, HuT's activities in Russia have grown steadily over the past decade, with evidence of HuT cells stretching from Tatarstan to Siberia.[25]

The growth in radical Islamic ideas has been accompanied by a surge in religiously motivated violence. In the summer of 2012, for example, Valiulla Yakupov, a prominent Islamic cleric who had previously served as the deputy spiritual head of Tatarstan, was shot and killed outside of his home in Kazan. Almost simultaneously, Ildus Faizov, the region's chief mufti, was injured by a bomb planted in his car.[26] Both men were well known for their active opposition to the spread of radical Islam and their work in preaching a more moderate, inclusive brand of the faith.[27] As such, the attacks represented a very public rejection of the established religious status quo in the region.

Tatarstan is not the only part of the Russian heartland locked in an intensifying battle with Islamic radicalism. Neighboring Bashkortostan—whose capital city, Ufa, serves as the spiritual seat of Muslims in eastern Russia—is also under siege. There has been a marked growth in grassroots Islamist militancy and widespread banditry in the region over the last three years.[28] This instability contributed to the ouster of the region's long-serving president, Murtaza Rakhimov, in the summer of 2010, and his subsequent replacement with a new, Kremlin-selected strongman, Rustem Khamitov. A new offensive against Islamic militants and ethnic separatists followed.[29] Nevertheless, sustained violence by both Islamists and extreme nationalists became so acute over the following year and a half that in December 2012, the Kremlin took the unprecedented step of dispatching internal security forces to quell the instability—the first time it had done so since the fall of the Soviet Union.[30]

For years, experts such as Yana Amelina and Rais Suleymanov of the Russian Institute of Strategic Studies and Gordon Hahn of the Center for Strategic and International Studies, have warned of the growing influence of Wahhabis in the region.[31] To them, the steady growth of radical Islam is part of a deepening struggle for the soul of the Russian state—a struggle that Moscow has not yet begun to fight in earnest.

HARD POWER, NOT SMART POWER

The rise of Islamic radicalism in Russia underscores the bankruptcy of the Kremlin's approach to counterterrorism. Russia's leaders long have gambled that their counterterrorism policies, however bloody, would remain popular so long as ordinary Russians believed the Islamist threat to be both marginal and distant. Yet numerous high-profile terrorist incidents in recent years—including the 2002 hostage-taking at Moscow's Nord-Ost theater, the 2004 Beslan school massacre, the 2009 bombing of the Moscow metro, and the 2011 Domodedovo attack—have increasingly made that gamble look like a losing one.

Why have Russian efforts to combat Islamic radicalism failed? Much of the problem lies in the way Moscow conceptualizes its struggle with Islamic forces. Indeed, while some in Russia recognize the need for an "intellectual war" against Islamic extremism,[32] the Kremlin's approach remains overwhelmingly kinetic. The Russian military's engagement in the Caucasus over the past two decades can best be described as a scorched-earth policy that has left more than a hundred thousand citizens dead. (In 2005, an unofficial Chechen estimate placed the combined death toll from the two Chechen wars at 160,000.[33] Official tallies offered by Moscow are more modest.)

Belatedly, the Kremlin and regional governments have begun to try a softer approach that includes greater economic investment in the Caucasus and outreach initiatives designed to engage, and moderate, regional Islamists.[34] But the brutality of Russia's hard-power policies have overshadowed these steps and led to widespread disaffection with Moscow.

The feeling is increasingly mutual; as the Carnegie Moscow Center's Alexei Malashenko has put it, most Russians have come to see the Caucasus as their "internal abroad"—an area qualitatively different from the rest of Russia, which must be pacified rather than engaged.[35]

Runaway regional corruption plays a large role in this hostility. The Russian government has come to rely on a succession of

Kremlin-approved strongmen to maintain local order in its majority-Muslim republics—and to preserve their allegiance to Moscow. It has also subsidized most of their expenses; estimates suggest the Kremlin currently provides between 60 and 80 percent of the operating budgets of regional republics such as Chechnya.[36] But accountability and transparency have lagged far behind. Not surprisingly, corruption and graft have proliferated, and the Caucasus has gained global notoriety anew for its criminality and lawlessness.

In response, Russian officials have proposed an array of remedial measures intended to make regional governments more transparent and accountable.[37] Yet these steps remain mostly notional; experts say that substantive changes to entrenched cronyism are hard to find.

The Kremlin's response to Islamism has been particularly feeble in Russia's heartland. Despite the warning signs, there is still little official recognition from Moscow that the country's heartland is fast becoming a battleground between insurgent Islam and the state, much the way the North Caucasus did some two decades ago. In December 2012, for example, Fariz Askerzade, the head of Tatarstan's Shi'a community, penned an open letter to Russian president Vladimir Putin beseeching him for protection against rising Islamic radicalism in the region.[38] He's still waiting for an answer.

This passivity has been encouraged by regional officials, who have been quick to reassure the federal government and the general public that radical Islamic activism remains "under control."[39]

THE CENTER CANNOT HOLD

For years, the Russian state has waged unrelenting ground warfare against Islamist elements on its periphery instead of implementing a real, broad-based strategy to combat and compete with radical Islam. Such an approach, however, is unsustainable.

Although Russia has experienced a post-Soviet religious revival, observance among Russian Muslims today remains limited—a legacy of the Soviet Union's forcibly imposed atheism and religious repression. According to Russian studies, just one-fifth of the country's ethnic Muslims actively practice the faith.[40] And among those who do, support for Islamism is not widespread.[41]

But the Kremlin's policies have the ability to change all that. As Ariel Cohen of the Heritage Foundation puts it, "Russia's entire counterinsurgency strategy is in question. Its primary goal is 'to make the local population less afraid of the law enforcement than the insurgents,' but the overly violent Russian approach has often produced the polar opposite."[42] Moreover, experts caution against underestimating the resilience—and the appeal—of radical religious ideas. "All this talk of Abkhazis, Ossetians or Tatars not being predisposed to major Islamism is nonsense," Moscow-based scholar Yana Amelina maintains. "Unfortunately, all [of them] are susceptible to radical Islamist ideology."[43]

Even more crucial, time is working against Moscow. Negative demographic trends have hit Russia's Slavs the hardest, while Russia's Muslim population is thriving. The practical effect is that the Russians most adversely affected by the Kremlin's draconian counterterrorism policies—the country's Muslim underclass—are the ones emerging as the most decisive demographic group and important political player in Russia's future.

CHAPTER FIVE

THE FAR EAST FLASH POINT

n July 2000, newly elected Russian president Vladimir Putin made
an official trek out to the country's distant Far East. He went there
to deliver a stark warning. "If you do not take practical steps to
advance the Far East soon," Putin told an audience in Blagovesh-
chensk, a wind-swept city of two hundred thousand souls situated
on the banks of the Amur River, opposite China, "after a few decades
the Russian population [here] will be speaking Japanese, Chinese and
Korean."[1]

The new president was encouraging his countrymen to come to
terms with a sobering reality: in the country's resource-rich east,
which serves as its economic engine and the repository of its

prodigious energy wealth, the Russian state is receding. The People's Republic of China, meanwhile, is advancing, both economically and demographically.

At the time Putin issued his candid assessment, the number of Russians living in Siberia and the Far East (a territory of more than four million square miles)[2] stood at twenty-eight million—merely 19 percent of the country's overall population.[3] But the latest Russian census, carried out in 2010, pegs the number of citizens in Siberia and the Russian Far East at just 25.4 million—or fewer than six inhabitants per square mile.[4] By contrast, the population density in China's Heilongjiang province, opposite the Russian regions of Amur, Khabarovsk, Primorskii Krai, and the Jewish Autonomous Region, is approximately thirty-five times that: between 210 and 220 citizens per square mile.[5]

And the disparity is growing. The negative population trends evident elsewhere in Russia—high mortality, low birth rates, and massive emigration—are also affecting its Far East. Although the area accounts for more than a third of Russia's territory, the Far East remains an economic and political backwater—one that until very recently garnered little attention from the Kremlin.[6]

But if Moscow has neglected the Far East until now, the same cannot be said of Beijing. China's political, economic, and demographic footprint in Russia's east is large and expanding.

UNEASY NEIGHBORS

There is historical precedent for China's interest, and for Russia's concerns. In fact, the two countries have contested much of the area for centuries. Its status as a Russian holding is relatively new—and increasingly fragile.

Until the seventeenth century, the territory of today's Far East remained largely unpopulated, claimed at times by the Russian Empire and at others by warring Chinese clans. In 1689, the Treaty of Nerchinsk—signed to end fighting between the Qing Dynasty and Russian settlers in the Amur Valley—granted control of much of the area to China. But successive centuries saw Russia begin to populate the region in earnest, solidifying its claims through a series of treaties (specifically the Treaty of Aigun in 1858 and the Treaty of Peking two years later). China never fully accepted Russian claims to the Far East, but the barrenness of the territory and its distance from the seat of Chinese power in Peking conspired to keep the conflict muted. The two countries would continue to contest the territory, however, even engaging in an isolated military skirmish along the Amur River in 1969.[7]

It was not until the 1980s, when Soviet Russia and Red China began a process of political reconciliation, that real progress began to be made on resolving the status of the Far East. By the late 1990s, nearly all of the outstanding territorial disputes between the two countries had been resolved (largely in Moscow's favor). The remainder was formally ended in 2001, when Moscow and Beijing inked the Treaty on Friendship and Good Neighborliness.

That twenty-five-point agreement, signed with great fanfare in Moscow in July 2001 by Chinese President Jiang Zemin and Russian President Vladimir Putin, was intended as a codification of a new era of Sino-Russian cooperation—and a manifestation of their shared desire for "multi-polarity" and a diminution of America's global influence.[8] But the treaty, like Russian-Chinese cooperation itself, is temporary. Despite Russian requests for an agreement of indefinite duration during the negotiating process, the Chinese insisted on a time limit for the deal. That demand was incorporated into the final text of the agreement that was signed by Jiang and Putin, and said treaty now formally "sunsets" in 2021.

The implication is clear. Looking two decades ahead in 2001, Beijing believed that the demographic balance between itself and Russia, and the larger bilateral strategic relationship, would be quite different. By 2021, with population trends working in its favor, China might well want to revisit its presence in the Far East with an eye toward reclaiming lost lands.

A CREEPING CHINESE ADVANCE

But the Chinese government may not be content to wait that long. In recent years, China has attempted to speed the process of Russia's decline, and its own advance, in the Far East.

For years, Russian experts have warned that Russia's eastern regions are being overrun by Chinese migrants.[9] While exact numbers are difficult to determine, estimates range from as many as 1.5 to 2 million Chinese nationals in Russia's Far East.[10]

The actual number is almost certainly much lower. A 2003 study by the American Foreign Policy Council estimated that there were fewer than 150,000 Chinese nationals throughout Russia's entire Far East.[11] A survey by China's state-controlled *People's Daily* the following year put the number of permanent, legal Chinese residents in Russia's East at between one hundred thousand and two hundred thousand.[12] Today, that number is considerably larger—about four hundred thousand by Western estimates—making clear that China's presence in the Russian Far East is increasing.

Some of that growth is a result of the thirty thousand Chinese tourists who visit the region daily. Tellingly, anecdotal evidence suggests that many of these visits are driven by more than simple curiosity; rather, many Chinese say they are returning to the region as absentee landlords looking after lost ancestral lands.[13] Not surprisingly, some of these tourists do not return home.[14]

Chinese also make up a major part of the Far East's labor force. The economies of the Far East's regions are oriented overwhelmingly toward China.[15] It only stands to reason, then, that they would rely heavily on Chinese workers to fuel that trade. And they do: in 2006, some 210,000 Chinese were legally registered to work in Russia—ten times the number registered in 1994.[16] Most reside in the Russian Far East. (The number of illegal Chinese migrant workers, which is not regularly tallied by Russian authorities, makes the actual size of the Chinese labor force in Russia larger, perhaps substantially so.)

This growth of Chinese migration to Russia is at least partly a product of China's expanding economy (which has averaged a stunning pace of 10.5 percent annually since 2007).[17] Beijing must now create twenty-five million jobs annually to keep its unemployment rate static.[18] This requirement has led the Chinese government to encourage labor migration abroad, to Latin America, elsewhere in Asia, in Africa—and to neighboring Russia. China's local governments have also encouraged labor migration to the Far East.[19]

Meanwhile, the Far East's desolation and its distance from European Russia generally (and Moscow specifically) have reduced

Russia's indigenous workforce. During Soviet times, Communist Party restrictions on citizen mobility kept the Far East's population in place. But a post-Soviet relaxation of travel regulations has prompted an exodus from Russia's desolate east. Since the Soviet collapse, an estimated two million Russians have departed the region, most for economic or social reasons, taking much of the area's labor with them.[20] By some estimates, the region has lost as much as one-fifth of its total population over the past two decades.[21]

Those who have remained aren't exactly the best and the brightest. "The Russian labor force in the Far East of the country is highly marginalized," explains Natalia Zubarevich, director of regional programs of the Independent Institute for Social Policy. "Those people are presumably alcoholics who do not have high working skills. Moreover, this force is very expensive against the background of the Chinese."[22] In other words, Russia has lost the comparative labor advantage to China on its southeastern flank.

Finally, China is winning the investment battle. The resource-rich Russian Far East has become a hub for Chinese commerce—a free-wheeling marketplace where China's hungry entrepreneurs are pressing their luck. In recent years, savvy Chinese investors have succeeded in setting up special economic zones in places such as the Amur Region, the Jewish Autonomous Region, Primorye, and Khabarovsk.[23] Investment dollars have followed; in 2011, Chinese speculators poured $3 billion into projects in Russia's Far East—more than three times the amount of money allocated by Moscow.[24]

While much of the Chinese migration to Russia's Far East is legitimate, some of it is undoubtedly happening illegally. Today, there is a consensus among Russian officials that many Chinese nationals live in Russia. Where they disagree is on how many there actually are—and whether their presence is a threat to Russian security.

In response to the influx of Chinese in the Far East, Russia has attempted to curb—or at least control—the movement of Chinese nationals into its territory. It has done so by shortening the number of days allotted on work visas for Chinese visitors; requiring official sponsors for these individuals in both Russia and China; and increasing official searches for illegal Chinese migrants.[25]

Russia has also instituted protectionist policies aimed at limiting the ability of Chinese workers to settle and prosper within the Russian Federation. In September 2012, for example, Russia's Amur Region followed in the footsteps of cities such as Krasnoyarsk, Chelyabinsk, and Nizhny Novgorod and banned Chinese migrant farmers from cultivating land there in the future.[26]

But the trend line appears relentless. The demographics of the Russian Far East are slowly changing. And, despite the various exclusionary efforts of Russia's regional governments, they are changing in China's favor. As a 2006 study of the subject in the *Asia Times* put it, "Chinese expansion is [now] a fact of life in the Russian Far East, and there is little Russia can do to stop it."[27]

HIGH STAKES

The transformation now underway in the Far East could help determine Russia's economic well-being—and its aspirations on the world stage. In recent years, the ongoing economic crisis in Europe, as well as Russia's growing political tensions with Eurozone countries, has prompted the Kremlin to look east for new markets to aid its domestic modernization, secure new economic opportunities, and help restore its status as a great power.[28]

By necessity, Russia's resource-rich Far East looms large in this calculus. The region has been likened to an "energy superpower"— an area with vast, and as yet largely untapped, hydrocarbon wealth. Indeed, the island of Sakhalin alone is estimated to have deposits totaling fourteen billion barrels of oil and 2.7 trillion cubic meters of natural gas.[29] Other resources, from softwood lumber to natural gas and precious metals, are also abundant. Yet although Sakhalin and other parts of Russia's east have become a magnet for foreign— including Western—investment, the endemic culture of corruption that permeates virtually every aspect of post-Soviet society in Russia has deterred more conservative investors and slowed economic development.

The Kremlin understands this. President Putin has declared publicly that the modernization of the Far East—and, by extension, a closer linkage with Russia's "federal center"—represents the "most important geopolitical task" facing Russia.[30] His government has matched its words with economic investments. Over the past decade, the Russian government has made a concerted effort to invest in the Far East. In 2007, it launched a "Federal Targeted Program" for the Far East and Trans-Baikal regions, earmarking $22 billion for their development.[31] Two years later, it went even further, implementing a new strategy that envisioned a three-stage process of development that would dramatically increase regional economic productivity by 2025.[32]

But despite these steps, real, broad-based development of the Far East remains mostly a dream for a simple reason. For all the lofty rhetoric, Russia's plans depend heavily on corresponding investments in the area from neighboring Asian nations.[33] And so far, none have economically engaged Russia's east. None, that is, except China.

COOPERATION NOW . . .

The conflict over the Far East is not yet at the forefront of relations between Moscow and Beijing. For the moment, improving bilateral diplomatic, economic, and military cooperation remains a cardinal priority for both countries.

These ties are driven in part by fears of Western encroachment. Back in 1997, Alexei Arbatov, then chairman of the Military Commission of the Duma, Russia's lower house of parliament, expressed this concern explicitly. If the United States and its allies used NATO to continue to press in on Russia from the west, Arbatov warned, Russia, too, would have to look east—to new partners in Asia.[34] And look east Moscow did. In 1997, Russian president Boris Yeltsin and Chinese premier Jiang Zemin issued a joint communiqué emphasizing the need for "multipolarity" in global affairs—a thinly veiled reference to joint opposition to America's perceived post–Cold War hegemony.

Since then, the Sino-Russian partnership has expanded significantly. For example, Russia has pledged to side with the PRC in the event of a conflict over Taiwan—one of China's primary national security priorities. In the summer of 2000, President Putin told President Jiang that the Russian Pacific Fleet stood ready to "block the path of U.S. naval vessels heading to Taiwan" if war ever broke out between the island nation and Mainland China.[35]

Moscow backed up its support with concrete strategic assistance. In 2004, the United States–China Economic and Security Review

Commission and the Pentagon both reported that Russia had sold China sophisticated weaponry as part of the latter's preparations for a conflict in the Taiwan Strait.[36] The following year, China and Russia launched their first ever joint military exercises in the Yellow Sea, staging a mock invasion of a third country in a not-so-subtle simulation of a takeover of Taiwan.[37] Russia has also supported China in opposing Taiwan diplomatically. When then Taiwanese president Chen Shui-bian called a referendum over the island nation's bid to join the United Nations, Russia equated the move with "dangerous splittism." Owing at least in part to Moscow's opposition, the UN ultimately rejected Taiwan's effort.[38]

Russia and China have also banded together to erect an anti-Western partnership in Central Asia. In 2003, the two countries jointly launched the Shanghai Cooperation Organization (SCO)—a six-member bloc incorporating the Central Asian states and designed at least in part to serve as a counterweight to NATO and the United States in the post-Soviet space. While the immediate goals of the bloc are to strengthen counterterrorism and military coordination among member states, the geopolitical objectives are clear. The SCO, China's official *People's Daily* has explained, gives member states "the ability and responsibility to safeguard the security of the Central Asian region"—and to demand "Western countries to leave Central Asia."[39]

Military cooperation between the two countries has blossomed as well. In the 1990s, the Russian government, seeking to capitalize on the lucrative remnants of Soviet militarism amid turbulent post–Cold War economic times, sold many high-tech arms to China. By 1997, close to half of Russia's foreign military sales (approximately $2 billion a year) went to China.[40] By the early 2000s, that figure had grown to $4 billion annually under a five-year plan negotiated by Moscow and Beijing. In the process, Moscow, in the words of one analyst, became "Beijing's 'logistics base.'"[41]

Bilateral trade has risen dramatically. Throughout the 1990s, Moscow and Beijing enjoyed strong political ties, but weak economic ones, averaging between $5 and $7 billion annually as a result of Russia's post-Soviet political instability.[42] But the 2000s saw a massive surge in economic cooperation between the two countries. By 2011, trade had rocketed to $83.5 billion a year.[43]

And Russian and Chinese officials are seeking still more growth; at their summer 2012 summit, Russian president Vladimir Putin and his Chinese counterpart, Hu Jintao, codified the ambitious goal of more than doubling trade—to $200 billion annually—by the end of the decade.[44]

This cooperation is not without its detractors. A decade ago, Russian nationalists such as the late General Alexandr Lebed pointedly warned that their government's policy of high-tech sales to China could lead to a growing strategic imbalance between the two—one that would put Moscow at a profound disadvantage if it and Beijing ever ended up going to war.[45]

Nevertheless, the long-standing consensus in Moscow remains that strategic cooperation with China serves a concrete, and financially rewarding, purpose. And because it does, the future of strategic ties between Moscow and Beijing is bright—or so it would seem.

. . . BUT COMPETITION LATER

Yet for all of the fanfare that has accompanied the Sino-Russian strategic partnership in recent years, there is a clear sense that today's era of bilateral cooperation will not last. China, after all, is a rising power, in both economic and political terms. Russia, by contrast, is declining, Kremlin dreams of an economic resurgence in Asia notwithstanding.[46] Given this dynamic, the lure of an empty, resource-rich territorial expanse on its borders could well prove irresistible to the PRC in the not-too-distant future.

Russian officials understand this very well. Even if they tend not to say so publicly, fears of Chinese encroachment are never far from the minds of Russia's elites. Thus, Sergei Karaganov of Russia's Council on Foreign and Defense Policy warned recently that the Russian Far East could "turn into an appendage of China" unless Moscow gets serious about reversing the PRC's advance on its eastern periphery.[47] Russia's leadership thinks much the same. In the summer of 2012, Prime Minister Dmitry Medvedev himself warned about the need to protect the Far East against "excessive expansion by bordering states"—a clear reference to China's growing clout in the area.[48]

The Russian government is doing what it can to prevent—or at least delay—this encroachment. In the spring of 2012, a national development paper entitled *Strategy 2020* prepared for Vladimir Putin's return to the presidency focused for the first time on the need to counterbalance China economically.[49] Shortly thereafter, in May 2012, the Kremlin authorized the establishment of a dedicated ministry to oversee development of the Far East.[50] That ministry, established by presidential decree and headed by Victor Ishayev, the Kremlin's special envoy for the development of the Far East, is a long overdue sign of seriousness on the part of the Russian government about the need for major, sustained economic and political attention to its distant eastern periphery.

But it faces an uphill battle. Chinese investments in Russia's Far East far outpace those of the Russian government and are likely to do so for the foreseeable future. So do demographic trends, which clearly favor a rising (and resource-hungry) China over a declining Russia.

Given these realities, the Kremlin has begun to plan for the worst. In June 2010, Russia's defense ministry launched "Vostok-2010," a massive war game in the Far East and Siberia. The weeklong drills, which involved some twenty thousand soldiers from Russia's army, navy, air force, and special WMD detachments, were unprecedented in their scope and aimed at ensuring what military officials termed, generically, "the security of national interests of the state in the Far East."[51] Some observers, however, had a more somber reading of the drills and the motivations behind them. "Russia is conducting these operations to reassure itself it can still control these sparsely populated regions," respected Russian military analyst Alexander Golts told reporters at the time.[52]

Vostok-2010 was just the beginning. In the three years since, Russia has significantly beefed up its military presence and command structure in the Far East under the banner of military reforms. The Russian military's Eastern Command, headquartered in Khabarovsk, now controls the country's Pacific Fleet, the Far East, and most of Siberia, making it a veritable beachhead against potential Chinese incursion.[53] It has also deployed advanced military hardware, including units of its advanced S-400 air defense system, to the Far East.[54]

The implications are clear. For all of its public praise of the Sino-Russian partnership, Moscow sees its future with Beijing as one of competition and not cooperation. The Far East will be the front line of this future conflict, with Russia's territorial integrity and its natural resource wealth the ultimate prize. Those are high stakes indeed.

CHAPTER SIX

PUTIN'S CRUMBLING STATE

Fifteen years after he strode onto the Russian national scene, Vladimir Putin is beginning to show signs of weakening power. Although he handily won reelection to the Russian presidency in March 2012, switching places with his handpicked protégé Dmitry Medvedev (who assumed the post of prime minister), Putin now finds himself facing eroding popularity and a mounting sense of political siege.

The numbers tell the story. A February 2013 poll by the Levada Center in Moscow found that only 32 percent of Russians would vote for Putin if elections were held today—a drop of nearly ten percentage points from June 2012.[1] Over the same period, the number of those who would choose not to vote at all rose to nearly a quarter of all respondents.

Putin's plunging popularity is easily explained. Dmitry Medvedev's presidency (2008–2012), during which time Putin served as prime minister, was viewed with optimism by some in Moscow (and more than a few in the West). That hope was misplaced because, despite his dulcet tones and talk of reform, Medvedev made few tangible alterations to Russia's political direction. This stasis culminated with Putin's preordained return to the presidency in March 2012—a development that sparked widespread disaffection and mass protests throughout that year.[2]

In a democracy, such political numbers would be fatal to a president's political future. Even in authoritarian Russia, they are deeply worrying to the Russian president and his coterie. As a result, the Kremlin has launched a number of initiatives to tighten its grip on power, even as it attempts to project the image of a more pluralistic and accountable polity.

POTEMKIN POLITICS

Following his rise to power in the last days of 1999, Putin set about consolidating Russia's then unruly political scene. A key element of that effort was the creation of United Russia, a pro-Kremlin political faction built upon the Unity Party that dominated the country's 1999 parliamentary elections.

In the years that followed, United Russia became a dominant force in Russian politics, securing commanding majorities in Russia's 2003 and 2007 parliamentary elections as well as in various regional and local political contests. Recently, however, the bloom has come off United Russia's political rose. In the 2011 Duma elections, it failed to win even half of the popular vote—a testament to the party's flagging popularity.[3]

As a result, Putin has begun to think bigger. Since 2010, his administration has attempted to build a broader political coalition—one that rehabilitates United Russia while simultaneously diminishing its opponents. The result, unveiled by Putin in May 2011, is the "All-Russian National Front," a grand coalition of parties, organizations, and "non-affiliated United Russia supporters" designed to help the president's political faction formulate a political platform and seed its candidates throughout parliament.[4] Today, the "National Front" unites hundreds of national and regional political and social groups under a pro-Kremlin umbrella.[5] That bloc is closer than ever to becoming the unquestioned hegemon in Russian politics. Russian experts have projected that, by the fall of 2013, the National Front will become the dominant force in the Russian Duma.[6]

The Kremlin has similarly sought to transform the workings of Russian politics. In May 2012, a series of reforms championed by Dmitry Medvedev during his time as president were signed into law. Kremlin supporters contend that these steps—which include, among other things, a lowering of the political bar on the registration of political parties—reflect a new reality in which the Russian government is increasingly forced to take into account the views and wishes of the electorate.[7]

But more objective observers are not so sure. They point to the fact that the Putin government continues to wield broad discretion over the legitimacy of political candidates and parties. As such, they say, Putin's recent policies—however pluralistic they appear at first blush—are simply more of the same heavy-handedness.[8]

The Kremlin's treatment of Russian civil society groups tends to confirm the latter view. Worried over the "color revolutions" that have taken place in the post-Soviet space in recent years and wary of the prospects of something similar occurring in Russia, the Russian government has assumed a dramatically harder line toward nongovernmental organizations.

Among the measures enacted by the Kremlin is a notorious "foreign agent law" that forces nongovernmental organizations that receive funds from abroad to register with the country's Justice Ministry as "foreign agents" and provide quarterly accounting of their activities.[9] The move was seen by civic activists as a concrete step designed to silence dissent.[10] These fears appear to have been realized: using the law as justification, the Russian government in recent months launched what observers call an "unprecedented" campaign to investigate the activities of thousands of NGOs active in the Russian Federation.[11]

The end result is that Putin's Russia, while on paper nominally more free, is functionally less so. Rather, it is a modern-day political version of a Potemkin village: an artificial construct designed to mollify the masses with the form of pluralism but without the substance of it.

ROTTEN TO THE CORE

In the heady early days of post-Soviet Russia, President Boris Yeltsin spoke out publicly against the economic and political disorder plaguing his country. Russia, Yeltsin said in 1994, had become "the biggest mafia state in the world ... the superpower of crime that is devouring the state from top to bottom."[12] Fast-forward almost two decades, and the situation in principle is substantially different—but in practice is eerily similar.

Over the past dozen years, the Putin government has focused on consolidating and centralizing power, transitioning first to a system of "managed democracy" and from there to a highly hierarchical authoritarian state. This has, by necessity, entailed a reining in of Russia's ubiquitous and powerful criminal entities.

Today, organized criminal groups, once unaccountable, operate under a new code—one in which they are mindful of, and in return receive exceedingly soft treatment from, the Kremlin.[13] Putin's government likewise has clamped down on Russia's powerful oligarchs, conveying to them in no uncertain terms that they enjoy their wealth and freedom at the pleasure of the Kremlin, and that political cooperation is the key to preserving both. The result is a micromanaged investment climate deeply hostile to entrepreneurship and dominated by capricious government policies.

International business has taken notice. Capital flight from the Russian Federation has surged as multinational corporations and investors have abandoned the country's uncompromising economic atmosphere. In 2010, for example, $33.6 billion left Russia. In 2011, that figure more than doubled, totaling $84.2 billion—and leading to a notable weakening of the Russian ruble.[14] In 2012, that figure dipped to $56 billion, but experts maintain that Moscow has made little real progress in addressing the underlying socioeconomic conditions fueling such flight.[15]

These conditions include organized corruption on a staggering scale. According to a February 2013 study by research group Global Financial Integrity (GFI), Russia lost more than $200 billion in illicit financial outflows stemming from crime, corruption, and tax evasion between 1994 and 2011. All told, the study estimates "the size of Russia's underground economy—which includes, among other things, drug smuggling, arms trafficking, and human trafficking—at a massive 46% of GDP" over that period.[16] These figures are a tragedy for ordinary Russians. "Hundreds of billions of dollars have been lost that could have been used to invest in Russian healthcare, education, and infrastructure," GFI Director Raymond Baker points out.[17]

On the surface, the Russian government seems to be addressing the issue. During his presidency, Dmitry Medvedev called it "one of the most dangerous and most serious problems" in the country and took steps to destroy Russia's culture of corruption.[18] One move was the 2008 creation of an advisory body known as the Anti-Corruption Council; another was the 2012 launch of the Open Government Initiative—a "roadmap" for stemming corruption and increasing governmental transparency.[19] These initiatives ostensibly have been inherited by the Putin administration.

The Kremlin's initiatives have claimed a number of casualties. In November 2012, long-serving Defense Minister Anatoly Serdyukov was publicly sacked by the Kremlin over his purported role in the speculative sale and illegal transfer of government assets totaling millions of dollars.[20] Subsequently, in early 2013, Vladimir Pekhtin, a lawmaker from United Russia, was forced to vacate his seat in the Russian Duma after an opposition blogger disclosed that Pekhtin possessed multi-million dollar properties in Florida.[21] Pekhtin was the second Duma deputy to be stripped of his parliamentary immunity in less than a year.[22]

But these high-profile examples, observers caution, do not reflect a broader commitment by the Kremlin to eradicate corruption.[23] Indeed, the very foundations of Putin's state—and, by extension, his hold on power—rely on loyalty that is secured through informal dealings and graft. Without them, the Putin government's hold on power would quickly loosen.

Increasingly, the same also holds true for another key node of power in post-Soviet Russia: the Orthodox Church.

AN "ORTHODOX IRAN"

In February 2013, Russian president Vladimir Putin took to the airwaves to make an unprecedented public declaration of faith. Standing alongside Kirill II, the patriarch of Russia's Orthodox Church, at a press conference in Moscow, he told the assembled reporters that the "Russian Orthodox Church and other traditional religions should get every opportunity to fully serve in such important fields as the support of family and motherhood, the upbringing and education of children, youth, social development, and to strengthen the patriotic spirit of the armed forces."[24]

Putin's statement was a monumental reversal. For most of the Soviet past, the Russian Orthodox Church had been relegated to the margins of the USSR's formally atheist politics (although it did play a role in shoring up the legitimacy of the Soviet Communist Party among the country's population). Today's relationship between church and state in Russia is much deeper, more overt, and more visceral. Simply put, the Kremlin has come to view the Church as an ally, and a tool with which it can tighten its hold on power and the people.

The Russian Church, for its part, has become increasingly comfortable with this new relationship. And, even as Putin's government has given the Church more space to influence Russian society, it has wasted no time doing so. Over the past two years, Russia's patriarchate has weighed in on everything from education to morality.[25] It has also pressed the faithful to embrace Putin's political agenda—and to reject those of others.

The Church's politicking has netted results. In the spring of 2012, for example, a group called the Public Committee on Human Rights issued a blacklist identifying fifty-five "anti-Christian xenophobes" active in Russian political life. Among those identified as being guilty of "blasphemy" were former chess champion (and staunch regime opponent) Garry Kasparov, human rights crusader Lev Ponomaryov, and internet activist and blogger Alexei Navalny.[26] The message was clear: being an opponent of the Russian government increasingly is synonymous with being an apostate.

This support, in turn, has informed the Russian government's draconian treatment of Pussy Riot, a punk rock group that in March 2012 performed an inflammatory anti-Putin concert at Moscow's Christ the Savior Cathedral. Three of the band's members were arrested after the show, and two of them were sentenced to two years' incarceration in a prison camp for hooliganism aimed at inciting religious hatred.[27]

The Russian government's infusion of power into the Orthodox Church has been so dramatic that opposition figures like Boris

Nemtsov have taken to warning publicly about the dangers of Russia turning into an "orthodox Iran"—a country where clerical fiat stifles political and cultural life.[28]

Indeed, the trend line is ominous. In the early 1990s, Russia formally recognized thirty-one religious denominations. But most were largely legislated out of existence in the years that followed. Today, in a throwback to Soviet practice, only four religions—Russian Orthodoxy, Islam, Judaism, and Buddhism—are formally recognized by the Russian government. And with the Kremlin's help, the Orthodox Church is rising in power and prominence.

Not surprisingly, this has exacerbated already-tense relations between the Russian state and its growing Muslim minority. In line with American philosopher Eric Hoffer's famous dictum that ideologies are inherently competitive,[29] the Russian Church—imbued with Kremlin's support—is beginning to crowd out other forms of religious identification in Russia. And it is doing so at precisely the time when the bonds holding the country's various ethnicities together have become more tenuous than ever.

ENERGY DOMINANCE ... FOR NOW

In March 2002, Russia officially became the world's top energy producer, for a time eclipsing Saudi Arabia in oil production. The event was the culmination of a goal that had animated the Kremlin since the collapse of the USSR: to reemerge as a global energy superpower.

It would be hard to overstate the importance of energy on Moscow's strategic agenda. "Energy is Moscow's primary tool of foreign

policy influence and attempted dominance," notes Janusz Bugajski
of the Center for Strategic and International Studies in Washington.
"[A]nd the Kremlin has systematically undertaken to become the
leading energy superpower in Eurasia."[30] It has done so "either by
controlling pipelines from Eurasia to Russia and then Europe or by
maximizing its control of gas supplies from Russia (including those
Central Asian supplies) to Europe."[31]

Energy represents far more than an economic instrument for the
Russian government; it is also a geopolitical weapon and a tool of
strategic dominance. To that end, Russia has pursued a variety of
energy maneuvers throughout Eurasia over the past decade. It has
opposed some projects (such as the Baku-Tbilisi Caspian oil route
during the 1990s), undermined others (such as the ill-fated Nabucco
natural gas pipeline to Eastern Europe), and derailed still others
(including the Odessa-Brody pipeline connecting Ukraine to Poland).
It has also successfully nurtured an unhealthy dependency on its
energy exports among European countries. As of 2010, nearly half
of Europe's natural gas imports came from the Russian Federation,
making some countries on the continent deeply vulnerable to any
manipulation of supply that might take place in Moscow.[32]

Russia has been able to do all this in large part because of its
status as a bona fide energy superpower. Russia, the U.S. Department
of Energy estimates, "holds the world's largest natural gas reserves,
the second-largest coal reserves, and the ninth-largest crude oil
reserves."[33] Russia is therefore in a league of its own in the production
and exportation of both natural gas and oil.[34]

But despite its resource wealth, Russia risks being left behind by
the global energy scene. The problem is practical: experts estimate

that, at its current rate of production, Russia has thirty years of proven oil reserves and sixty years worth of proven natural gas reserves.[35] This energy wealth has made Moscow resistant to the idea of energy diversification, and the Kremlin has neglected to explore and harness alternative and renewable sources of energy. (In the United States, by contrast, something resembling a "revolution" in shale gas is now taking shape, with momentous consequences for U.S. energy independence and its position vis-à-vis foreign oil suppliers.)[36]

Russia has also failed to make substantial investments in the infrastructure it needs to remain a global energy power. Its 2002 foray into the role of the planet's top energy producer was short-lived; by the following year, Russia's energy output had receded, in part due to a crackdown on high-profile figures and firms by the Kremlin (chief among them energy conglomerate Yukos and its head, Mikhail Khodorkovsky). The Kremlin's heavy-handedness toward its energy sector had a chilling effect on foreign direct investment into Russia.[37] But shoddy infrastructure—and a lack of serious investment in the same by the Russian government—likewise had constrained the country's energy horizons. In a 2004 interview with Interfax, then Economic Development and Trade Minister German Gref admitted as much when he told the state news agency that the country's oil production had plateaued and was expected to rise by less than 5 percent annually for the foreseeable future.[38]

Nearly a decade later, not much has changed. The Russian government recently pledged a whopping $1 trillion in funds to develop the country's infrastructure. But, observers in Moscow say, these funds are intended overwhelmingly for the rehabilitation of basic infrastructure (such as roads and bridges across the Russian Federation's sprawling expanse). Upgrades to Russia's energy facilities and pipeline grid are not likely to be forthcoming.[39] And because they are not, Moscow has been forced to look further and further afield for new energy-rich arenas to preserve its global position.

NORTHERN EXPOSURE

In recent years, no region has preoccupied Russian attention in terms of energy more than the Arctic. Over the past decade, climatological changes have made more and more of the previously inhospitable region accessible to oil and natural gas exploration, with dramatic results. According to the U.S. Geological Survey, the Arctic seabed may hold as much as ninety billion barrels of oil and a third of the world's untapped natural gas reserves.[40] These findings have sparked renewed interest from oil companies, as well as from the "Arctic Five" nations—Canada, Denmark, Norway, Russia, and the United States—whose borders abut the region.

But in Moscow the new findings have done much more. Russian policymakers' hopes for an energy renaissance depend on the Arctic, and they have made the acquisition of a greater stake in the area a cardinal national priority. Then President Dmitry Medvedev said as much in September 2008, when he told a meeting of his National Security Council, "[o]ur first and main task is to turn the Arctic into a resource base for Russia in the 21st century."[41]

Since then, the Kremlin has set about crafting a legal framework for dominating the region. It has done so because the Arctic lacks its own legal regime, relying instead upon the rules and regulations contained in the 1972 UN Convention on the Law of the Sea (UNCLOS). Under them, each of the "Arctic Five" nations is allowed to stake a claim to roughly two hundred miles of Arctic territory beyond its demarcated northern border. (The rest is considered part of the "global commons," over which no nation can claim sovereignty.)

Moscow has cited UNCLOS in its expanding claims to the region. Over the past decade, it has asserted that the so-called Lomonosov Ridge, a massive undersea geological formation in the Arctic Ocean, is part of its sovereign continental shelf and, therefore, that it is solely entitled to its resources. (That position is contested by Canada and Denmark, which claim to have evidence that the Ridge is rightly part of the North American continent.) In 2007, Russia even sent an expedition to the North Pole to plant an undersea flag on the Ridge as proof of its territorial claim.[42]

But Moscow has also attempted to refashion the region's geopolitical order to reflect its own interests. In March 2009 it publicly released the full text of its new Arctic strategy, entitled *The Foundations of Russian Federation Policy in the Arctic until 2020 and Beyond*.[43] That document, first issued in September 2008, lays out a dramatic expansion of official Russian sovereign interests in the area. According to the strategy, the Arctic zone represents "a national strategic resource base" for the country—one that is "capable in large part of fulfilling Russia's needs for hydrocarbon resources." As such, Russia must systematically develop the region and create "a system of complex security for the defense of the territories, population, and objects in the Arctic zone of the Russian Federation critically vital to Russian national security from threats of a natural and technical character."[44]

Russia has moved forward with these objectives. Economically, it has encouraged large-scale and sustained investment in the region on the part of Western multinationals such as BP, as well as Russian firms (including state natural gas giant Gazprom). Militarily, Moscow has worked to make the region its own exclusive strategic purview. In 2011, the Russian Ministry of Defence announced plans to station two army brigades in the Arctic in order to expand Russia's presence in the region and "defend its interests" there.[45] It has also begun construction on a fleet of new submarines to better "protect Moscow's interests in the icy North."[46] And in early 2013, Russian warplanes began regular patrols of the Arctic Ocean.[47]

For the time being, officials in Moscow have discussed the need for multilateralism in managing the Arctic.[48] But the strategy that Russia has adopted over the past half-decade is unilateral and increasingly aggressive. It is no wonder that more than a few people now fear that an "Arctic cold war" might be imminent.[49]

TROUBLE AHEAD

Although it appears consolidated from the outside, Putin's state today rests on unstable foundations. These systemic flaws have forced Russian authorities to adopt an increasingly repressive and authoritarian approach at home.

But this situation has the potential to become much, much worse. For, although the effects may not be immediately apparent to casual observers of Russian politics, the demographic, political, and ethnic trends at work within the country's borders are already threatening its internal stability, as well as its relationship with the world.

CHAPTER SEVEN

MISUNDERSTANDING THE MUSLIM WORLD

In October 2003, in a move that went mostly unnoticed in the West, Vladimir Putin traveled to Kuala Lumpur, Malaysia, to attend the annual summit of the Organization of the Islamic Conference, known today as the Organization for Islamic Cooperation (OIC). Putin's mission was clear. As he told the assembled delegates, "Russian Muslims are an inseparable, full-fledged, and active part of the multiethnic and multi-denominational nation of Russia."[1] Accordingly, the Russian president said, his government should be granted observer status in the fifty-seven-nation bloc.

Although Russia's request was denied at that time (it was granted in 2005), Putin's voyage was nonetheless significant. It signaled a concrete recognition by the Kremlin that Russia is, or soon will be, an "Islamic state."[2] The fact that it was carried out despite significant opposition from entrenched elites in Moscow—from the *siloviki*, members of Russia's security and armed forces whom Putin saw as his traditional power base, to the oligarchs that had grown rich from the country's energy sector—made it all the more telling.[3]

RUSSIA'S RETURN

It also represented a historic reversal. For much of the past century, Russia's relationship with the Islamic world has been both complex and acrimonious. During the Cold War, the Soviet Union attempted to engage a variety of anti-Western regimes and actors in the Middle East, from Saddam Hussein's Iraq to Yasser Arafat's Palestine Liberation Organization. It had some success, mostly thanks to the efforts of Yevgeny Primakov, the wily spymaster who served as the KGB's point man for the region during the 1970s and 1980s.[4] But the Soviet Union's atheist ideology, and its 1979 intervention in Afghanistan—an act that prompted the world's first global *jihad*—made it a focal point of Muslim anger throughout much of the USSR's later years.

The Soviet Union's withdrawal from Afghanistan, and its subsequent dissolution, reconfigured Moscow's relationship with the Muslim world, which was quick to embrace the five majority-Muslim republics of Central Asia. Russia, however, remained a problem, with the conflict in Chechnya drawing significant ire from Islamic states in the Russian Federation's first years. During the same period, a pro-Western foreign policy (championed by then foreign minister

Andrei Kozyrev) helped to relegate Russia to the sidelines of regional politics.[5]

But beginning in the mid-1990s, the removal of Kozyrev, and his replacement with hard-line Arabist Yevgeny Primakov, reestablished Russia's imperial and anti-Western approach to the region. "The world is moving toward a multipolar system," Primakov explained to *Rossiyskaya Gazeta*, a Russian government daily, shortly after his installation as foreign minister. "In these conditions we must pursue a diversified course oriented toward development of relations with everyone ... [and] we should not align ourselves with any particular pole."[6] For their part, more than a few Middle Eastern countries—increasingly discontented with Western policy—turned to Russia as a political balancer and alternative to America and Europe in the region. Moscow thus reverted to (mostly) Soviet behavior.

Over the past decade and a half, Russia has progressively assumed the role of balancer and pro-Arab broker in the long-running peace negotiations between Israel and the Palestinians. This includes support for the Palestinian Authority's (PA) participation in regional forums, including Arab League summits,[7] as well as serving as a consistent backer of the PA's bid for international recognition at the United Nations.[8] Moscow has simultaneously pivoted toward support for the more radical elements of Palestinian politics, undermining Western diplomacy by unilaterally engaging with the Hamas movement.[9] It has done so despite warnings by Russian experts that the Kremlin's outreach to Palestinian radicals was at odds with its approach to the breakaway republic of Chechnya—and that this double standard could end up damaging Russia's image in the eyes of moderate Muslims.[10]

Russia also expanded its role as a key strategic partner and political enabler of Saddam Hussein's regime in Iraq—a relationship that continued until Saddam's ouster by Coalition forces in 2003. At that time, oil and drilling contracts held by Russian companies were estimated to be worth nearly $44.1 billion.[11] Over the course of Saddam Hussein's regime, half of Iraq's arms came from Russia. So did shipments of electronic jamming equipment, night vision goggles, and anti-tank weapons, provided in violation of UN sanctions.[12]

In 2003, a cache of captured documents revealed that Moscow was even sharing intelligence with, and providing training for, Iraq's intelligence operatives.[13] With Saddam's removal, however, Moscow found itself progressively shouldered out of political developments in the former Ba'athist state. Its massive economic stake in Iraq—developed during the decades of Saddam's rule—was largely nationalized by Iraqis who saw Russia as a foe because of its backing of the *ancien régime*. It took the Kremlin years to reestablish a commercial foothold in the country.

And today, Russia's standing in the Muslim world has been progressively undermined by its strategic ties to two countries.

EMBRACING IRAN

In Moscow's Mideast policy, no country matters more than Iran. Over the past three decades, Moscow and Tehran have formed a major partnership—one that so far has endured both September 11 and the expanding global crisis over Iran's nuclear program.

The contemporary Russo-Iranian entente can be traced back to the collapse of the Soviet Union, which unleashed a wave of ethnic and religious separatism in Russia's turbulent "southern rim" of Central Asia and the Caucasus and raised the prospect of Iranian interference there—something Moscow was eager to mitigate. Russia saw practical reasons for the partnership. Its defense industry had not weathered the post-Soviet transition well, and Iran—then emerging from a ruinous eight-year war with neighboring Iraq—promised to be a significant source of income for the battered Russian armaments sector. (One leading expert would later admit that Russia "should be grateful to Iran for having provided tens of thousands of Russian companies with 70 percent of their work.")[14] The resulting arrangement between Moscow and Tehran during the 1990s included a pledge of Russian sales of conventional arms (and later the sharing of nuclear know-how) to Iran in exchange for a tacit understanding that Tehran would steer clear of meddling in Russia's near abroad.

Under the stewardship of Vladimir Putin, this partnership has strengthened yet further. In November 2000, in a public show of support for the Iranian regime, Russia officially abrogated the 1995 Gore-Chernomyrdin Agreement, under which Moscow had agreed to curtail new nuclear-related exports to the Islamic Republic. The importance of Russia's ties with the Islamic Republic also became a feature of the foreign policy blueprint issued by the Russian Foreign Ministry that same year.[15]

Despite the events of September 11 and the ensuing War on Terror, ties between Moscow and Tehran remain strong. Over the past several years, fears of a long-term Coalition presence in Eurasia (fanned by U.S. and allied activity in Afghanistan, Iraq, and Central Asia) have led Moscow and Tehran to begin discussions of a common political and security agenda for the post-Soviet space.[16]

Nuclear cooperation likewise continues, with Russian officials supporting Iran's atomic effort in the face of mounting international concerns.

Yet this does not mean that Russia trusts Iran. Many Russian experts believe that the Islamic Republic could someday soon pose a real threat to their country. Officials like Andrei Kokoshin, the influential chairman of the Russian State Duma's Defense Committee (and a former Russian National Security Advisor), and Alexei Arbatov, leader of Russia's liberal "Yabloko" political faction, have publicly questioned the prudence of their country's partnership with the Islamic Republic.[17] So has Yevgeny Velikhov, the secretary of Russia's Civic Chamber and the country's top nuclear scientist.[18] Indeed, today, the view that Iran cannot be allowed to acquire nuclear weapons is increasingly common among officials in Moscow.[19]

Yet cooperation with Iran's ayatollahs continues to be seen as necessary, for both practical and strategic reasons. Officials in Moscow are wary of severing ties with an increasingly capable Islamic Republic, and emphasize the need to maintain good relations with neighboring states.[20] Indeed, Iran's ability to stir up trouble on Russia's periphery, or within Russia's own restive Muslim regions, remains a real concern for policymakers in Moscow.[21] As a result, Moscow has sought to keep the Iranian regime pacified—and peaceful—through economic and diplomatic outreach.

Trade with Iran also remains a boon to Russian industry. In the years after September 11, Russia's vast energy sector—and the high world price of oil—helped fuel the country's revival. Since the onset of the global financial crisis in late 2008, however, Russia's economic fortunes have faded. Paradoxically, Iran's nuclear program has provided a bit of assistance in this regard. Since Iran's nuclear program broke into the open, there has been an explosion of interest in the atom in the greater Middle East, with at least fourteen countries in the Middle East and North Africa openly beginning to pursue some level of nuclear capability.[22]

Russia, the world's leading exporter of nuclear technology, has capitalized on this trend, inking nuclear cooperation deals with a number of these nations, including Algeria and Jordan.[23] Russia's conventional arms trade has benefited, too. Growing international concerns over Iran's nuclear program has led to an upsurge in investments in arms and defenses in the already volatile Middle East. According to the Stockholm International Peace Research Institute, arms sales to the region rose by nearly 40 percent between 2004 and 2008, with Iran's neighbors among the most active clients.[24] As a result, Russia's arms industry is now in the midst of a major expansion in the Middle East.[25] In other words, Iran's nuclear program has turned out to be very good for Russian business.

Strategically, meanwhile, Iran helps Russia to further a key geopolitical priority: continued hegemony over its near abroad. Officials in Moscow are deeply worried over the encroachment of the United States and its NATO partners into the post-Soviet space. These fears were made explicit by NATO's formal declaration at its June 2004 Istanbul summit that it plans to expand its activism and involvement in Central Asia and the Caucasus,[26] and by the so-called color revolutions that have taken place throughout the post-Soviet space in recent years.

Iran provides a way out. A West preoccupied with containing and managing a crisis in the Middle East, the thinking goes, is far less likely to meddle in Russia's traditional sphere of influence. The West likewise will be unable to seriously challenge Russian efforts to reassert its dominance over parts of the former Soviet Union, either politically (as in the case of Ukraine) or militarily (as in Georgia, for example). This, in turn, has reinforced Russian convictions about the prudence of cooperation with the Islamic Republic.

STANDING BY SYRIA

Russia's second major regional partner is Syria. Relations between the two countries date back to the Soviet era, when the USSR saw Hafez al-Assad's regime as its most durable and lucrative client state. Indeed, from his rise to power in 1971 until the early 1980s, Assad ran what scholars have termed "the most consistently pro-Soviet state in the Middle East,"[27] building a formidable arms and strategic dialogue with Moscow. (Thereafter, the outbreak of Syrian hostilities with Israel chilled its external relations, at least for a time.) A centerpiece of that partnership was a 1971 agreement to house the Soviet navy's Mediterranean flotilla in the Syrian port city of Tartus.[28] The Syrian regime also became a major consumer of Soviet arms. By the end of the Soviet era, Syria's debt to Moscow was estimated to have totaled a whopping $9 billion.[29]

Strategic ties survived the collapse of the USSR. In fact, after a brief weakening in the early Yeltsin years, they grew stronger, as Moscow came to see its partnership with Damascus as part of a counterweight to U.S. policy in the region.[30] This focus was reinforced in subsequent years by the Clinton administration's repeated efforts to engage Syria as part of the Middle East peace process—efforts that the Kremlin vociferously opposed.

The 2000 death of Hafez al-Assad held out the promise of a Russo-Syrian divorce—and of a Syrian rapprochement with the region at large. But Bashar al-Assad, Hafez's son and successor as president, chose to maintain the status quo. This included perpetuating Syria's strategic relationship with Moscow. Between 2000 and 2010, Damascus acquired roughly $1.5 billion in arms from Russia, making Syria Moscow's seventh-largest contemporary arms client.[31] This was made possible in large part by a 2005 agreement that wrote off the bulk of Syria's debt to Russia, providing some much-needed relief to the Syrian economy.[32] In exchange, Syria has continued to serve as a staunch ally of the Kremlin and to provide its navy with vital access to the Mediterranean.

The Russia-Syria relationship has deepened still further since the outbreak of the Syrian civil war in March 2011. Moscow has greatly aided the brutal campaign of repression Assad is waging against his own people. It has continued to provide Damascus with critical arms and weaponry—matériel that has been used against the Syrian opposition.[33] Russia likewise has run interference for Syria at the UN Security Council, complicating international efforts to create a durable coalition by which to pressure the Assad regime to end the war.[34] And, despite mounting evidence of a fundamental rupture between Assad and his domestic opposition, Moscow consistently has sought a political solution that would preserve the Syrian strongman's hold on power.[35]

ADRIFT IN THE ARAB SPRING

In late December 2010, a Tunisian street vendor named Mohamed Bouazizi, frustrated over being prohibited by government functionaries from peddling his wares, set himself ablaze as a sign of public protest. The spark ignited a popular protest in the North African country, inciting demonstrations that forced the resignation of the country's long-serving president, Zine al-Abidine Ben Ali, in January 2011. From there, the Arab Spring spread to Egypt. That month, popular protests erupted against the rule of Hosni Mubarak in Cairo, leading the Egyptian president to step down in February 2011 after roughly three weeks of street clashes and political disorder.

Like Western nations, Russia was caught off guard by the rapid changes taking place in the region and as a result hewed a cautious foreign policy line toward the political transformations taking place in Tunis and Cairo.[36] But the outbreak of unrest in another North African country, Libya, caused a significant rupture between Russia and the West.

There, the resilience of Muammar Gaddafi's regime and the growing prospects of a civil war in the country progressively provoked discussion of Western intervention. The Russian government strongly opposed such a course of action, warning of its destabilizing potential.[37] Western nations nonetheless went ahead, and the eventual outcome, the ouster of Gaddafi's regime and his death at the hands of rebel forces, infuriated Russian officials, who saw it as a violation of NATO's supposed neutrality.

It was also a tangible economic blow, since Gaddafi's Libya owed Russia some $4.5 billion in debt, which Moscow now appeared to have to write off.[38] Ongoing arms sales and infrastructure projects worth billions of dollars were also called into question, significantly increasing Russia's potential losses.[39] Russia thus aggressively pursued and secured new arms contracts with Afghanistan and Oman, as well as countries outside the greater Middle East (such as Ghana and Tanzania).[40]

This policy, Russian officials argue, is both prudent and pragmatic. Since the outbreak of the Arab Spring, Islamist forces have been gaining momentum from Mali to Egypt. These changes, as seen from Moscow, threaten important Russian interests and allies in the Middle East. They also have the potential to represent a mortal threat to the Russian Federation itself, insofar as Islamist tendencies could further mobilize Russia's already-restive Muslim minority. As a result, Moscow has pursued outreach as a way of "controlling through investments," as one former Kremlin official puts it.[41]

Yet Moscow's approach has increasingly placed it on the wrong side of the Arab Spring—and of the Muslim world writ large. Moscow has become embroiled in a civil war that is taking place within Islam itself because its two principal Middle Eastern allies, Syria and Iran, are both Shi'a Muslim states (although the former only loosely so), while the rest of the Muslim world is overwhelmingly Sunni (who make up some 85 percent of the planet's 1.57 billion Muslims). As a result, Russia is now pursuing what one official in Moscow says amounts to an "accidentally Shi'a" policy in the Mideast.[42] And in response, Russia's regional image has plummeted precipitously.

Just how much was illustrated by the late 2012 announcement of Yusuf Qaradawi, a spiritual leader of Egypt's Muslim Brotherhood and arguably the most influential Sunni cleric alive, that "Moscow has become the enemy of Islam and of Muslims these days."[43] Qaradawi's comments augur ill for Russia's standing in the Middle East, where its policies—although historically consistent—have begun to make Moscow a pariah among the countries of the Arab

Spring. But they could easily also portend Russia's future, particularly if the Kremlin's Middle East policy becomes a rallying point for Russia's own radicalizing Muslim masses, or if the narrative of Russia as an enemy of the Sunni world is exploited by Islamist forces seeking to mobilize them.

But the Middle East is not the only place where the Kremlin is losing ground. Despite crafting an ambitious strategy to emerge as an Asian nation in recent years, Russia now finds itself in retreat there as well.

CHAPTER EIGHT

IN RETREAT IN ASIA

In early 2012, the Obama administration went public with a major shift in defense and foreign policy focus. "U.S. economic and security interests are inextricably linked to developments in the arc extending from the Western Pacific and East Asia into the Indian Ocean region and South Asia, creating a mix of evolving challenges and opportunities," the policy planning document unveiled by then Defense Secretary Leon Panetta noted. "Accordingly, while the U.S. military will continue to contribute to security globally, we will of necessity rebalance toward the Asia-Pacific region."[1] Since then, the so-called "pivot" to Asia has consumed American strategic priorities on many levels.

But the United States is hardly the only nation to have fixed its attention on the Asia-Pacific of late. A number of other countries have begun similar turns to the East. The list includes the Islamic Republic of Iran, which views Asia as an economic and strategic lifeline in the face of mounting Western sanctions over its nuclear program.[2] But Russia also ranks high on the list of Asian aspirants. Since at least mid-2010, the Kremlin has made a similar shift to the East a major focus of its own foreign policy.

WHY THE KREMLIN COVETS ASIA

It has done so for practical reasons. The instability that accompanied the 2008 global economic downturn has made Europe, Russia's traditional trading partner and arena for commerce, less lucrative and attractive than it once was for Moscow. The Asia-Pacific, Russian policymakers contend, has replaced Europe as the engine of global economic growth. Thus the region is valuable to Russia because it houses "[new] markets for energy, raw materials, technology, [and the potential for] new areas of bilateral and international cooperation."[3]

Asia, moreover, is increasingly seen in Russia as a safer investment bet than is Europe. "Asian countries are … leaders in terms of gross savings, which actually determine an economy's investment potential," a July 2012 study by the influential Valdai Discussion Club points out. "China is far ahead of others here (20.7%). Other Asian countries included in the top ten are Japan (3rd), India (5th) and South Korea (10th). These four countries together account for 34.5% of global savings."[4]

Russia's interest in Asia has been reinforced by Moscow's increasingly problematic relationships with Europe. Over the past decade, energy diplomacy and extensive business interests have significantly broadened Russia's stake in the EU, and vice versa. But political ties between Moscow and European capitals remain fraught. They were only made worse by European disappointment over Vladimir Putin's return to the Russian presidency after what many in Europe had hoped would be a period of liberalization during the tenure of his protégé, Dmitry Medvedev.[5] (More recently, the economic turmoil that has proliferated in places such as Greece and Cyprus, where Russia's oligarchs maintain considerable assets and interests, has convinced more than a few Russian policymakers that their high degree of investment in Europe constitutes a distinct liability.)[6]

Strategic problems also abound. Russia today has rising conflicts with the West on a wide array of issues. Foremost among these is missile defense. Russia has vociferously opposed NATO plans to erect a Europe-wide anti-missile capability to defend against rogue state ballistic missile threats (such as the one from Iran). It has rejected Western assurances that the shield is not meant to neutralize the Russian Federation's strategic arsenal and has attempted to use the issue to divide Europe and the United States. "Progress toward genuine partnership between Russia and the North Atlantic alliance is still being hampered by attempts to exploit the Soviet threat idea, which has turned into the Russian threat idea now," Russian foreign minister Sergei Lavrov told audience members at the forty-ninth Munich Security Conference in February 2013. "Even during a shortage of financial resources, we can see increasing military activities in the north and the center of Europe, as if threats to security were growing in these regions."[7]

This acrimony has persisted despite the efforts of European capitals and the White House to alleviate Moscow's mistrust. Even the Obama administration's March 2013 announcement that it plans to table the fourth phase of its European Phased Adaptive Approach—on which the NATO shield depends—due to budgetary considerations appears to have done little to mollify the Kremlin.[8]

These disagreements and a host of others—over Moscow's continued support for the Assad regime in Syria, its continued military presence in Georgia, and the country's deepening domestic drift toward authoritarianism—have led Europe to increasingly rebuff Russia's diplomatic and commercial advances.[9] In response, Russia has sought to distance itself from Europe in favor of greener economic and political pastures in Asia.

All politics is ultimately local, however, and Russia's shift toward Asia has a distinctly domestic component as well. Some two-thirds of Russian territory is located in Asia, making a tilt toward the East intuitive (if not necessarily politically desirable among many in "European Russia"). Russian officials, moreover, increasingly have focused on the Far East as a gateway to global prominence. "The main potential for Russia becoming an Asia-Pacific power lies within its own boundaries," a recent Valdai Club study notes—to wit, the massive expanses of arable land and abundant renewable resources (such as lumber and water) available in Siberia and the Far East.[10] Indeed, the report concludes, "[i]t would be no exaggeration to say that Russia's regions east of the Urals and in the Far East are the last 'virgin lands,' one of the few regions left in the world fit for arable farming that are still a long way off being fully exploited agricultur-ally."[11]

This potential, the thinking goes, has the ability to make Russia indispensable to the countries of the Asia-Pacific and a global player in a new arena.

AMBITIONS, NOT STRATEGY

Yet, beyond the atmospherics, Russia's turn toward the region is still mostly notional. A "long-term and comprehensive Asian strategy is yet to be devised," Sergei Karaganov, one of Russia's preeminent political scientists, has admitted.[12] Privately, senior Russian diplo-mats share that view and see the Putin government's push into Asia as a political "exaggeration."[13]

However intuitive Russia's entry into Asia might be, such a step is far from assured. Russia has made some inroads into the region in recent years. At a 2010 bilateral summit, for example, South Korea pledged to significantly increase its imports of Russian natural gas, and Seoul's state-owned Kogas has since proposed the construc-tion of three pilot liquefied natural gas plants in Russia's region of Primorski Krai and on Sakhalin Island.[14] Two years later, Russian state-controlled gas conglomerate Gazprom inked a notional deal with the Japanese government to build a $13 billion natural gas terminal in the Russian Far East city of Vladivostok as part of the Kremlin's efforts to expand energy sales to Asia.[15] Russia even has begun to explore expanded ties to Myanmar (formerly known as Burma); in 2007, the two countries agreed in principle to the Russian construction of a light water nuclear reactor on Burmese soil, and

Burmese nuclear scientists are rumored to have been trained at Russia's nuclear institutes for more than a decade,[16] although concrete steps toward a real strategic relationship have yet to truly materialize.

In the main, however, Russia's regional footprint can still be considered small. "[B]y degree of involvement in the Asia-Pacific economy Russia is second lowest among APEC countries—only ahead of Papua-New Guinea," note Timofei Bordachev of Russia's National Research University and Oleg Barabanov of Moscow State University. "The Russian Far East is virtually absent from the economic map of the region. The other Asia-Pacific countries see no need to turn to Moscow for a discussion of various free trade zone projects."[17]

This is true institutionally as well. With the exception of APEC, Moscow exhibits a comparatively modest diplomatic presence in the region. It participated in the East Asia Summit as an observer nation at the bloc's first meeting in 2005 but didn't receive full membership until comparatively recently—in 2011. Russia and the Association of South East Asian Nations, meanwhile, have had a formal diplomatic dialogue since the mid-1990s, yet robust trade and strategic ties are still lacking.[18] In other words, Russia, for all of its efforts, is still very much a newcomer in the region.

Politically, too, Russian policymakers lack a comprehensive approach to Asia. Rather, Russia has promoted the idea of what its Deputy Prime Minister Sergei Ivanov has termed "network diplomacy." Russia seeks "an extended partnership network" in the region, Ivanov told the 2011 Shangri-La conference in Singapore: one that relies on Asia's "existing structures and forums."[19]

Russia's Asia policy is also impeded by a series of disputes—chief among them its long-standing and acrimonious tug-of-war with

Japan over the Kuril Islands. The island chain has served as a source of tension between Russia and Japan for more than 150 years, with sovereignty changing hands between the two countries repeatedly (in 1855, 1875, and again in 1905). During World War II, the Soviet Union and Japan found themselves on opposite sides of the conflict. In the final days of the war, the USSR occupied the islands (as well as the territory of Sakhalin), and Japan subsequently ceded its rights to all but four of the islands (which Tokyo asserted were part of Japan proper). In 1956, a joint declaration between the two countries suspended the conflict and solidified Japanese sovereignty over two of the four. Competing claims over the remaining two islands, however, prevented the codification of a formal treaty.[20]

So the situation has remained. To date, Moscow and Tokyo have yet to sign an agreement ending their dispute over the islands. To the contrary, both countries have steadily hardened their positions, damaging bilateral relations in the process. Over the past half-decade, the dispute has become much more serious. In 2009, the Japanese parliament adopted a law declaring the islands to be national territory, unjustly usurped by Russia. The Kremlin responded by orchestrating a state visit by then President Dmitry Medvedev to the Kurils, leading Japan to recall its envoy to Moscow.[21] Russia has since mapped out an ambitious development program for the islands, partnering with China to create a common investment fund for the area that's worth $4 billion.[22]

The conflict is about more than mere territory. A lucrative fishing industry and prospective underwater oil deposits make the islands desirable for both countries. Their proximity to the Japanese mainland, moreover, makes the Kurils an important geostrategic outpost for Russia. The dispute has taken a toll on diplomatic relations between Tokyo and Moscow and has hampered serious Japanese investment in Russia's Far East—at least so far.

These factors have caused Russia to pursue a reactive policy in the region—one driven by self-interest and ignorance of regional realities. Moscow's goal in Asia, as elsewhere, is to balance American power and to expand its own room for regional political and economic maneuver under the banner of "multilateralism."[23]

Yet Russia's regional presence appears anything but permanent. Throughout the region, an emerging consensus holds that Russia's influence is on the decline and that Moscow soon will become a spent force in Asia.[24] That same consensus holds that, despite the Kremlin's best efforts, a Russian retreat from Asia is inevitable, as it is subsumed by a rising and increasingly assertive China.

A CHALLENGE FROM CHINA

Similar assessments increasingly predominate in Moscow. Over the past decade, China's explosive economic growth has fueled a surging demand for energy. As a result, PRC officials consistently have sought to forge an energy partnership with Russia. At the core of their plans is a pipeline to bring oil from Siberia to northern China by way of a spur around Russia's Lake Baikal. That route, which is expected to bring roughly three hundred thousand barrels of oil to China daily over the next two decades, went operational in January 2011. As of January 2013, it had delivered thirty tons of Russian crude to China, making Russia a significant energy provider to the PRC.[25]

But Beijing is seeking still more. China has made clear that it wants to absorb all of the available oil carried by Russia's Eastern Siberia Pacific Ocean pipeline once that energy route—now under construction—comes online circa 2014.[26] In the process, it has fanned fears among Russian policymakers that, if they are not careful, their country could easily end up becoming nothing but an "energy appendage" to an insatiable China.[27]

Yet Moscow is doing little of substance to alter this trajectory. Putin's government has pledged approximately $1 trillion through the end of the decade to modernize the country's aging infrastructure. But such investments, observers say, do not include infusions of capital into sectors such as health and human welfare[28]—investments that are sorely needed if Russia is to sustain and expand its presence in the Far East. And because Russia is not making these investments, its pivot to Asia remains a matter of aspiration rather than reality. It is, moreover, an aspiration that is harder and harder to sustain.

CHAPTER NINE

REBUILDING THE EMPIRE

In January 2013, Alexei Kudrin sat down for an in-depth interview with Germany's influential newsweekly *Der Spiegel*. The interview was noteworthy because Kudrin, a former finance minister, is one of very few people whom Russian president Vladimir Putin counts among his confidantes. In fact, even though he is no longer in government (having left the Kremlin in late 2011 to become dean of St. Petersburg University), Kudrin's political star is still on the rise, and some see him as a possible future prime minister. Kudrin's stature made the comparatively progressive ideas he espoused in his interview—about economic diversification and the need for greater democracy, free elections, and a real dialogue with Russia's political opposition—all the more surprising.

But it was Kudrin's comments about his country's ideological outlook that were perhaps most striking. "There is a widespread attitude that I call 'imperial syndrome,'" he lamented. "A sizeable number of Russians place their country above other nations and see neighboring countries as part of our zone of influence."[1]

IDEOLOGUES OF EMPIRE

Today in Russia, this yearning for empire is embodied in a collection of influential politicians and thinkers who extol the virtue of an expanded Russian state.

Among the most conspicuous is Alexandr Dugin. At first blush, the bearded fifty-one-year-old KGB archivist-turned-political-theoretician seems like an unlikely power broker in the rough-and-tumble world of Russia's identity politics. Yet more than a decade and a half after emerging in earnest onto Russia's post-Soviet political scene, Dugin remains influential. His extreme ideas about Russian greatness and the country's geopolitical destiny as an empire have greatly influenced Russia's political leadership—and, by extension, the country's foreign policy direction.

Since the mid-1990s, Dugin has become a noted political philosopher. A prolific writer, he has authored numerous books and articles about Russian nationalism, its foreign policy, and its place in the world. But the cornerstone of his thinking is elaborated in *Osnovi Geopolitiki* ("The Foundations of Geopolitics"), a rambling, 924-page treatise that lays out Dugin's strategy for recreating an anti-Western Russian empire.[2] The tome is a manifesto of sorts for renewed national greatness—and for the idea that Russia, as Dugin puts it, "cannot exist outside of its essence as an empire, by its geographical situation, historical path and fate of the state."[3] It is also an eloquent articulation of why, according to him, Russia and the United States are destined for global confrontation. "The strategic interests of the Russian nation," Dugin has written, "must be oriented in an anti-Western direction … and toward the possibility of civilizational expansion."[4]

But Russia cannot do so alone. In light of its current, diminished international stature, Dugin posits a series of strategic alliances—with Iran, Germany, and possibly even Japan—through which Russia can again achieve international dominance. These partnerships, Dugin believes, should be based on the common "rejection of Atlanticism, strategic control of the USA, and the refusal to allow liberal values to dominate us."[5]

Dugin's ideas have taken concrete form. In 2000, he presided over the creation of "Eurasia," a sociopolitical movement dedicated to the revival of the art of geopolitics—and to the idea of a "Greater Russia" stretching from the Middle East to the Pacific. Two and a half years later, Dugin's ideas were formally entrenched in Russian political discourse with the chartering of his "Eurasia Party," a political faction deeply supportive of President Vladimir Putin's foreign policy line. Today, he occupies the chairmanship of the Department of Sociology of International Relations at the prestigious Moscow State University, where he fills eager young minds with his ideas about Russia's geopolitical destiny.

Over the years, Dugin's influence has ebbed and flowed with the currents of Russian foreign policy. But he remains a figure to watch because his popularity represents a bellwether for Russia's relationship with the West, as well as its global aspirations. Today, Dugin is again prominent on the Russian political scene, featured regularly in the national media in support of Putin's plans for a Eurasian Union unifying Russia with Kazakhstan, Belarus, and Ukraine.[6] Most recently, he has even emerged as a voice for the Russian government on the international scene, penning a March 2013 editorial in the *Financial Times* urging the West to better "understand" (and accommodate) Putin's global efforts.[7]

Even more significant and politically relevant is Dmitry Rogozin. At one time the deputy chairman of the State Duma, the ultra-nationalist Rogozin has long argued that Russia's government needs to work toward a post-Soviet Union of Slavic peoples. In his book *We Will Reclaim Russia for Ourselves*, published in the late 1990s, Rogozin makes the case that the country "should discuss out loud the problem of a divided people that has an historic right to political unification of its own land." Russians, he contends, "must present ourselves with the problem of a union, no matter how unrealistic this idea is in today's conditions. And we must create conditions to result in the environment with which Germany dealt for forty years coming out united in the end."[8]

Rogozin has spent the years since putting this idea into practice. Since the early 2000s, he has served as the Kremlin's special envoy to a number of enclaves held or coveted by the Russian state, including Kaliningrad and Moldova's Transdniester region.[9] Between 2008 and 2011, Rogozin was Russia's ambassador to NATO, where he championed an increasingly assertive foreign policy line toward the post-Soviet space—one at odds with the objectives of the Atlantic Alliance.[10] Rogozin has risen to the rank of deputy prime minister in Putin's government, as well as to the head of the Military-Industrial Commission of the Russian Federation, which aims to "revive the country's military-industrial complex" and "strengthen the defense of our country."[11]

Rogozin's political prospects look even brighter. In Moscow, his name—like Kudrin's—is discussed as a potential successor to Putin should Russia's president decide to bow out of national politics several years hence and leave the Kremlin to someone cut from the same cloth.[12]

Such sentiments about Russia's future are not held exclusively on Russia's Right, however. Across the Russian political spectrum, thinkers have long been contemplating ways to reconstitute their country's international greatness.

Their ranks include the late, great literary giant and anti-Communist icon Aleksandr Solzhenitsyn, who in the 1990s argued in favor of the reconstitution of the Slavic nation. "The trouble is not that the USSR broke up—that was inevitable," Solzhenitsyn wrote in his 1995 book *The Russian Question*. "The real trouble, and a tangle for a long time to come, is that the breakup occurred mechanically along false Leninist borders, usurping from us entire Russian provinces. In several days, we lost 25 million ethnic Russians—18 percent of our entire nation...."[13] The optimal solution, according to Solzhenitsyn, was the reconstitution of a greater Slavic state encompassing "a Union of the three Slavic Republics and Kazakhstan."[14] Solzhenitsyn's ideas found a lot of resonance in the Kremlin—so much, in fact, that despite his dissident status the civic crusader was invited in 1995 to repeat his call for Slavic unity on the floor of the State Duma.[15]

This sort of thinking is also pervasive on Russia's Left. Even Anatoly Chubais, the liberal architect of Russia's pro-Western economic reforms during the 1990s, has weighed in in favor of Russia's imperial expansion. "It's high time to call a spade a spade," Chubais wrote in *Nezavisimaya Gazeta* in October 2003. "Liberal imperialism should become Russia's ideology and building up liberal empire Russia's mission."[16]

The implications are clear. Irrespective of political outlook, the allure of "greater Russia" continues to fire the imaginations of Russia's elites. Indeed, more than a few politicians seem to believe that their country, in the words of Dugin, "can be either great or nothing at all."[17]

So do ordinary Russians. The collapse of the Soviet Union—and the loss of the constituent republics in the Caucasus and Central Asia, as well as satellites in the Baltics and Eastern Europe—was deeply traumatic to Russia's citizens, who had grown accustomed to their country's status as a superpower (even if a deeply repressive one). The political and economic upheaval that followed during the 1990s only intensified that trauma.

The numbers reflect this thinking. For example, more than 70 percent of respondents in a 2005 poll by the Moscow-based Levada Center said that the unification of Russia with Ukraine would be a positive move.[18] Roughly 40 percent of those polled said that they approved of a union with Belarus—an idea that has been advocated by the Kremlin for some time.[19] What's more, people in at least some of the territory of the former USSR (including Belarus and eastern Ukraine) are still sympathetic to—and see themselves as a part of—Russia, in both ethnic and political terms.[20]

AN ENDURING IMPULSE

The Kremlin has set about making such a union a reality. In 2001, in a move that went largely unnoticed by the international community, it passed a law formally codifying the procedures and protocols by which the Russian Federation could be expanded.[21] That new law provides a legal framework outlining how new subjects could be formed within Russia and how others could be annexed to it.[22]

Two years later, Russia's Defence Ministry issued a new defense concept outlining a more aggressive posture toward Russia's "near abroad." That document, known colloquially as the "Ivanov Doctrine" for its principal architect, then Defense Minister Sergei Ivanov, instituted major changes to Russian military structure and force posture in order to better "protect and further Russian interests" in its zone of strategic influence.[23] It was a not-so-subtle signal that, after a period of retrenchment, Moscow's territorial appetite had again been whetted.

In this effort, Belarus, Russia's closest economic and geopolitical ally, has received the lion's share of attention. The idea of a formal union has been a fixture in relations between the two countries since Alexander Lukashenko rose to power in Minsk in 1994 on a platform of neo-Soviet nostalgia. His appeal was understandable; Belarus's ten million citizens are all Slavs, mostly Russian Orthodox in religious belief and generally oriented toward Moscow in their political outlook. This viewpoint was formally codified in a 1995 Treaty of Friendship, Good Neighborliness and Cooperation, which emphasized the "common historical experience" of the two countries, as well as their joint desire for "deeper integration."[24]

The years since have seen more than a dozen bilateral agreements on everything from military cooperation to easing customs barriers and even a formal union declaration in the late 1990s. But a real unification of the Russian and Belarusian systems has not taken place due to various disagreements over trade and energy issues and because Lukashenko himself likely understands that such a step would make him dispensable.[25] Nevertheless, relations between the two countries remain close, and pro-unification sentiments abound on both sides of the border.[26] So does the idea that Belarus's integration into the Russian Federation remains simply a matter of time, since, as the prominent political scientist Samuel Huntington once noted, the country is "part of Russia in all but name."[27]

Russia's relations with the other main territory that it covets are considerably more acrimonious. Ukraine holds a prominent place in Russian policy because of its historic role as an ancient seat of Russian power (and, more recently, as a Soviet holding), and because it continues to serve as a key transit point for Russia's energy exports to Europe. Although the common border between the two countries was settled in the late 1990s, many in Russia still cannot bear the idea of an independent Ukraine.[28]

As a result, the Kremlin has systematically worked to subvert democratic institutions, cultivate compliant political candidates, and resurrect a pro-Moscow political order in Kiev. This has proved to be complicated, however, because Ukraine is a country divided: the country's eastern provinces are dominated by a Russian Orthodox population sympathetic to Russia, while its Western oblasts overwhelmingly look to Europe and the United States. This divide played out in the 2004 "Orange Revolution," which saw a democratic outpouring—supported and sustained in the country's west—upset the traditional pro-Russian status quo in Kiev with the election of pro-Western candidate Viktor Yushchenko to the country's presidency. (Ukraine's eastern oblasts, by contrast, protested against the move, even unsuccessfully floating the idea of becoming an autonomous region.)[29]

The revolt was a concrete challenge to Moscow, which responded with a campaign to undermine the fledgling Yushchenko government. Within less than five years, Ukraine's pro-Western consensus had collapsed, torn apart by competing domestic political factions. What followed was a political reversal that ended in the restoration of Ukraine's pro-Moscow orientation.[30]

So the situation remains. Kiev's current government, headed by pro-Kremlin president Viktor Yanukovych, has once again adopted a friendly line toward Moscow, extending Russia's lease to the strategic naval base at Stevastopol and codifying a close energy association that posits Russia as the senior partner. And while a strong sense of nationalism continues to predominate throughout Ukraine, sympathetic attitudes toward the idea of reintegration are not absent; one-fifth of Ukrainians now favor the unification of their country and Russia into one state.[31]

PUSHING THE BOUNDARIES

Elsewhere, Russia took a major step in this general direction when it invaded neighboring Georgia in August 2008. The weeklong conflict was precipitated by the Georgian government's increasingly assertive policies toward two autonomous territories in the country's north, the regions of South Ossetia and Abkhazia. In Soviet times, both had enjoyed the anonymous status within the Georgian Soviet Socialist Republic. When Georgia declared independence from the Soviet Union in 1991, it took the two areas along with it despite strong pro-independence sentiments in both. A series of skirmishes followed, culminating in the creation of an uneasy status quo whereby both South Ossetia and Abkhazia maintained functional independence but *de jure* were part of the larger Georgian state.

That balance held until Georgia's "Rose Revolution" of November 2003, which ousted long-serving pro-Moscow strongman Eduard Shevardnadze in favor of opposition leader Mikheil Saakashvili. In the years that followed, Saakashvili's government tacked west, improving relations with the United States and Europe while simultaneously distancing itself from Moscow.[32] Relations with Russia deteriorated precipitously, culminating in Moscow's decision to use force to protect South Ossetia when the Saakashvili government attempted to take over the region during the summer of 2008.[33]

From the start, the conflict had a strong territorial character. Prior to Russia's invasion, more than half of South Ossetia's population of seventy thousand had accepted Moscow's offer of Russian citizenship. Thereafter, the Kremlin argued that it was acting to protect the rights of those citizens.[34] It did so; over the course of five days, Russia launched a large-scale ground offensive against Georgia, decisively defeating the Georgian military in numerous battles in the breakaway region and thereafter occupying multiple cities in the former Soviet Republic.[35]

Mediation by the European Union ended the conflict, but Russia's shadow continues to loom over Georgia. Under a 2010 agreement grudgingly agreed to by Tbilisi, Moscow is permitted to maintain two thousand troops at a base in South Ossetia—making the region a de facto military protectorate of the Russian Federation.[36] Russia likewise has laid plans to build a permanent naval base in Abkhazia for its Black Sea fleet, cementing its long-term strategic presence there as well.[37] As of September 2012, a part of Russia's Black Sea Fleet had been deployed to Ochamshire, Abkhazia as part of this effort.[38]

For their part, South Ossetia and Abkhazia have firmly ensconced themselves in Moscow's orbit. In the wake of the 2008 conflict, both regions declared their independence from Georgia—a declaration that Russia promptly recognized.[39] (Most of the rest of the world, by contrast, has not; today, South Ossetia and Abkhazia are recognized by just six and five member states of the United Nations, respectively.)[40]

The reverberations have been felt in Tbilisi. Although Saakashvili handily won reelection in 2008, his popularity plummeted thereafter, at least in part because Georgians grew increasingly weary—and wary—of their country's deeply acrimonious relationship with Russia. This internal discontent culminated in the ouster of Saakashvili's government by a pro-Kremlin bloc in late 2012—and real movement toward a strengthening of ties between Tbilisi and Moscow since.[41]

However brief, the incident represents more than a mere territorial skirmish. It was the first time that Moscow has attempted to use force to reclaim former territories (albeit indirectly) since the end of the Soviet era. And the outcome of the conflict has served to reward Russia's urge for territorial expansion—and whet its appetite for still more.

THE LOGIC OF "GREATER RUSSIA"

Moscow's interest in its former holdings is animated by more than imperial nostalgia. The historic yearning for forfeited territory is also bolstered by concrete socioeconomic calculations. To wit, policymakers in Moscow recognize that the addition of Belarus's ten million citizens to the Russian Federation would increase Russia's overall population by some 7 percent. The addition of Ukraine would do even more; ethnic Russians make up nearly 20 percent of Ukraine's forty-five-million-person population, and if even part of the country were to formally vote in favor of annexation, the number of Russian citizens would swell significantly. If additional territories that are currently coveted by Moscow—including parts of neighboring Georgia and Kazakhstan—were added, that number would be higher still, significantly bolstering the Russian Federation's flagging demographics in the process.

Today, in light of the decline of Russia's Slavic population and the rise of its Muslim minority, the reclamation of lost lands has evolved from an aspiration to something resembling a strategic imperative. A recent article in the influential *Literaturnaya Gazeta* explained it this way: "Russia as a sovereign unitary state can exist only as long as the state-forming Russian people, which support the unity of Russia, maintain an absolute majority in the population. The fewer the number of Russians, the lower their share in the population, the greater the chances of Russia breaking up into petty 'independent' [states]."[42]

In other words, if Russia hopes to survive, it will need to assume an increasingly aggressive posture toward its former holdings in the years ahead.

CHAPTER TEN

MANAGING THE END
OF RUSSIA

In March 2009, when the Obama administration's outreach to Russia was still in its infancy, America's chief diplomat made a major gaffe. Meeting in Geneva with her Russian counterpart, Foreign Minister Sergei Lavrov, then Secretary of State Hillary Clinton presented him with a symbolic red button, meant to signify the "reset" of bilateral relations then being advocated publicly by President Obama.

But the button was mislabeled. In a glaring error of translation, it was inscribed with the Russian word *peregruzka*, meaning "overload," rather than the correct term, *perezagruzka* (signifying a "reloading" or "rebooting" of affairs). Both Clinton and Lavrov were quick to laugh off the incident, but a significant message had inadvertently been sent.

A FAILED RESET ... AND AFTER

In the years since, the "reset" with Russia—which has emerged as a centerpiece of the Obama administration's foreign policy agenda—has followed a predictable, if disheartening, trajectory. On a number of tactical fronts, Moscow and Washington have indeed drawn considerably closer. In terms of strategic priorities, however, the two countries remain worlds apart.

Most concretely, Russia has become a major player in Coalition efforts in Afghanistan, assuming a key role in the U.S.-led effort there. Today, an estimated 60 percent of U.S. supplies to troops in Afghanistan arrive by air, road, or rail via Russian territory.[1] Indeed, it would be fair to say that Moscow has helped sustain the War on Terror's first front, even as America's deteriorating relationship with Pakistan has progressively closed off traditional supply routes. As of March 2013, in excess of 2,200 flights, carrying 379,000 military personnel and 45,000 cargo containers, are estimated to have transited Russian territory en route to the Coalition in Afghanistan.[2]

Russian assistance on this front, moreover, is expanding. In June 2012, the Russian government came to terms with NATO on a supplemental transit route through the Volga region.[3] The move is deeply symbolic, given that the area is home to some 40 percent of Russia's Muslim population. It also reflects an abiding self-interest: Moscow's assistance, scholars note, has been rendered not "because of its love for the West." Rather, it is because Russian leaders are deeply concerned over Afghanistan's continued role as an incubator of Islamic extremism—and cognizant of the fact that, left unaddressed, the threat could easily migrate to exacerbate ethnic and sectarian tensions within the Russian homeland as well.[4]

The two countries likewise have managed to revive their bilateral arms control dialogue, which remained moribund during the later years of the George W. Bush administration. In late 2010, over the objections of many in the U.S. Congress, the Obama administration concluded a new arms control framework agreement with the Russian government. That treaty, colloquially known as New START, was a strategic victory for Moscow, enshrining new bilateral reductions of nuclear arms in a formula that deeply favored the Russian Federation.[5] It also provided a concrete affirmation to Moscow elites that Russia still mattered to official Washington—a not-inconsequential thing for a country preoccupied with its own global status. New START looks to be just the beginning; since ratification of the agreement, the two countries intensified their discussions about additional strategic reductions.[6]

In service of the "reset," Washington has also rolled back its commitment to missile defenses in Europe. In September 2009, the Obama administration unveiled a new missile defense policy, dubbed the "phased adaptive approach," in which it abandoned its predecessor's commitment to deploy early warning radars and interceptors in Poland and the Czech Republic in favor of a more graduated, four-phase plan to protect American allies (and eventually the U.S. homeland) from ballistic missile attacks from rogue states.[7] But even that plan increasingly has come into question. At a summit in Seoul, South Korea, in March 2012, President Obama was accidentally captured on a microphone telling outgoing Russian president Dmitry Medvedev that he would have "greater flexibility" to negotiate over the shape of American missile defenses following his reelection to the U.S. presidency, which took place in November 2012.[8] A year later, incoming Secretary of Defense Chuck Hagel announced that budgetary constraints and a rethinking of strategic priorities in the White House had led to a scrapping of the European component of the phased adaptive approach, which would have helped NATO build a missile architecture for Europe.[9]

Russia and the United States also collaborate on an array of science and technology issues. In the aftermath of the Obama administration's 2011 decision to scrap NASA's space shuttle program, Russia has emerged as America's de facto gateway to manned space, providing U.S. astronauts with transportation to the International Space Station.[10] For the time being, at least, Russia seems both ready and willing to play that role. In March 2013, the Russian government codified plans to collaborate with the United States on space research through the end of the decade.[11] Other issues, from cyberwarfare to nuclear research, are likewise the subjects of quiet bilateral cooperation.[12]

Strategically, however, the "reset" rests upon very flimsy foundations. This is because it is overwhelmingly an expression of American political desires writ large (and those of the Obama administration in particular), rather than a true, deep strategic and ideological reorientation by both countries. Indeed, Russian president Vladimir Putin has said as much. In December 2012, as part of a major press conference in Moscow, he told reporters that "reset" was an American term and objective, rather than a Russian one. "Reset is not our word," Putin said, "We didn't see the need in it at all."[13]

Moreover, because the "reset" is an American, rather than a mutual, construct, even the tactical areas of cooperation that exist today could prove fleeting. Astute observers have noted that there will be fewer areas upon which Moscow and Washington can cooperate in the years ahead—most conspicuously, with the end of war in Afghanistan in 2014. As a result, disagreements are likely to become more prominent and the bilateral relationship as a whole more acrimonious.[14]

Indeed, ties between Moscow and Washington already appear to be fraying. A particular flash point has been the so-called Magnitsky Act passed by Congress and signed into law by President Obama in late 2012. The legislation, named after the Russian lawyer who died of medical complications in a Russian prison in 2009 after exposing massive government corruption, blacklists a number of Russian officials implicated in Magnitsky's death from traveling to the United States and accessing the U.S. banking system.[15] The bill has riled Moscow, which has responded with its own legislation, the Dima Yakovlev Law, which bans Americans from adopting Russian children.[16]

As a result, policymakers in Washington are actively rethinking America's relationship with the Russian Federation—and downgrading it. "The divergence of the United States' and Russia's core foreign policy objectives has left the White House with two strategic options," Leon Aron of the influential American Enterprise Institute has written.[17] The first amounts to a resetting of the "reset" policy on Washington's part—a quest for more, and new, areas of commonality between the United States and the Russian Federation that might prove more durable than the current batch of issues under bilateral discussion.

The second, however, is the idea of a "strategic pause" in relations with Moscow, and a reevaluation of U.S. priorities in the relationship.[18] Increasingly, official Washington appears to be pursuing the latter course. Despite ongoing diplomatic contacts between the two countries, mounting anecdotal evidence suggests that the Obama administration, having unsuccessfully tried engagement with the Putin regime, is now content to ignore it altogether.[19]

American policy may currently be in flux, but the direction it ultimately takes will be informed by a fundamental reality: the Russian Federation is in the throes of a monumental transformation, the results of which will determine whether Russia emerges as a true partner of the West—or a mortal danger to it.

FUTURE IMPERFECT

Tucked away in a busy corner of the Pentagon is a little-known bureau known as the Office of Net Assessment (ONA). Headed by Andrew W. Marshall, the legendary nonagenarian strategist who has advised every American president since Richard Nixon, it serves as the U.S. military's in-house think tank on a broad range of foreign policy and defense issues. ONA's specialty, however, is a very specific discipline: the study of "alternative futures," the different ways in which countries might respond to external and internal changes in an increasingly complex geopolitical environment.[20]

Russia is a country ripe for exactly this kind of study. Although the trend lines highlighted in the preceding pages may not be immediately apparent to casual observers of Russian politics, they are already exerting an inexorable pull on the country's political direction. And while it is impossible to predict with certainty exactly how Russia will evolve in the years to come, several scenarios are plausible.

A STRENGTHENED IMPERIAL IMPULSE

Today the quest for renewed national greatness continues to preoccupy Kremlin elites and ordinary Russians alike. As a result, Vladimir Putin's ongoing efforts to rebuild Russia's geopolitical status (through military modernization, regional hegemony, and a nurturing of anti-Americanism) on balance have proven popular at home, at least for the time being. But the Kremlin's current, "post-modern empire"—a web of influence and strategic dependencies extending throughout the former Soviet Union, into Europe and beyond—can go only so far. As depopulation ensues in earnest in the coming decades, the Russian government will be compelled to adopt an even more aggressive policy toward its former territorial holdings in the post-Soviet space, the Baltics, and Eastern Europe. This is likely to lead to new territorial conflicts along Russia's periphery, as Moscow increasingly seeks to replace its current virtual empire with a tangible one and thereby prevent, or at least delay, its demographic collapse.

A CHINESE FAR EAST

Russia's drive to absorb its former Soviet republics will be reinforced by its receding presence in the Far East. The area (which serves as a key part of the Kremlin's energy strategy and the centerpiece of its Asia policy) is already being transformed by China's relentless rise. Observers in Moscow note that China's strategy is not one of outright conflict and that as a result, Beijing is not likely to go to war over the Far East after the expiration of its 2001 territorial treaty with Russia some eight years hence.[21]

But even absent outright conflict, the PRC's growing political and economic influence in the area will make Chinese dominance there a political reality long before it becomes a formal one. This advance is nearly inexorable, driven as it is by China's internal economic imperatives—unless, that is, Russia is willing to fight for control of the territory. But, at least for the moment, the Kremlin does not appear to be prepared to do so. And because it is not, Moscow's grip over the country's distant east will continue to weaken over time, until it disappears altogether.

RUSSIA HEADS WEST (TERRITORIALLY)

The demographic trends now predominant in both "European" Russia and in the country's distant east mean that the current territorial boundaries of the Russian Federation are not sustainable in the long run. Internally, a massive migration is already beginning to occur. Ordinary Russians—once constrained by Soviet authorities in where they could live—are taking advantage of their newfound, post-Soviet freedom of mobility to move westward, and are doing so *en masse*. The inhabitants of the inhospitable Far East are moving across the Urals to "European" Russia, where greater economic opportunity (and more temperate climates) exist. Those in the country's west, meanwhile, are departing the nation altogether. As a result, several decades from now, the country known as Russia is likely to control a smaller territory overall, and its land mass is likely to be situated farther west.

ONE, TWO, MANY CHECHNYAS

A decade ago, it was still possible for the Kremlin to dismiss the Islamist insurgency raging in the North Caucasus as a distant and contained phenomenon. Today, it is not—because the conflict is spreading quickly. Russia is witnessing the beginning of a confrontation between a radicalizing Muslim population and the Russian state writ large. It is, moreover, an insurgency that will inevitably gain in strength in the years to come unless the Kremlin can craft a real, meaningful counterterrorism strategy.

So far, it has not. Instead, Russia's leaders have engaged in a hard-power campaign against Islamic radicalism, hoping that overwhelming force will pacify the country's restive republics. The failure of that approach is evident in rising Islamist violence in places like Tatarstan and in the proliferation of extreme Islam throughout the Eurasian heartland. This phenomenon will pose a growing challenge to the stability and legitimacy of the Russian state in the years ahead—a challenge complicated by Moscow's counterproductive and Shi'a-centric policy in the Muslim world, which will serve as yet another source of grievance for the country's growing Sunni minority.

A NEW RUSSIAN CIVIL WAR

Nearly two decades ago, Russian civic icon Aleksandr Solzhenitsyn lamented his country's status as a "torn state" on account of the territorial divisions that took place with the USSR's collapse.[22] Today, Solzhenitsyn's description is more apt than ever, but for a different reason. Russia is more divided socially than at any time in its modern history. The rise of Islamic radicalism, the influx of Muslim migrants from Central Asia, the rise of rampant xenophobia and racism, and the expanding power of the Russian Orthodox Church cumulatively have the potential to transform Russia into a latter-day Yugoslavia, a nation riven by ethnic violence and sectarian strife. The Russian military provides a snapshot of this phenomenon. Even as the country has become more ethnically diverse (and divided), the Russian armed forces have headed in the opposite direction—becoming more homogenous and rigid. They have also become increasingly ideological, with Russia's armed forces seeing themselves more and more as "protectors of the state" against threats to the nation's character and core values.[23] The groundwork for a future civil war in Russia, a violent contest for the soul of the Russian state that will be fought along religious and ethnic lines, is thus being laid.

■ ■ ■

None of these alternative futures is assured. But all are plausible, given the trend lines now visible within the Russian state and society. Each, moreover, holds significant implications for the West.

A Russia engulfed in civil or sectarian warfare could quickly become a threat to its neighbors and to the international community at large. So could an increasingly aggressive Russia bent upon fresh territorial conquests in Slavic parts of the former Soviet Union. Prospects for a Russo-Chinese conflict over the Far East should likewise not be taken lightly, since such a war would inevitably draw in neighboring Asian powers (and, quite possibly, the United States as well). The safety and security of Russia's strategic arsenal, meanwhile, could be affected by the emergence of organized Islamic separatism within the Russian heartland—or by the country's descent into protracted civil unrest. And if current demographic trends hold, decades hence Russia could become the world's first majority-Muslim nuclear superpower with a permanent seat on the United Nations Security Council, fundamentally reconfiguring the nature of the global order in the process.

THE KREMLIN AT THE CROSSROADS

"Russia," British prime minister Winston Churchill famously remarked in October 1939, during the opening days of the Second World War, "is a riddle, wrapped in a mystery, inside an enigma." The British leader was commenting on Soviet leader Joseph Stalin's surprising August 1939 decision to sign a non-aggression pact with Adolf Hitler's Third Reich. That move helped keep the USSR on the sidelines of the unfolding global conflict, much to the chagrin of the Allied powers—until Germany's grand betrayal in June 1941 dragged the Soviet Union into what is still known in Russia as the "Great Patriotic War."

Fast forward seven decades, and little has changed. More often than not, Western policymakers are at a loss to properly explain Russia's behavior and correctly characterize its relationship with the world. In large measure, official Washington still clings to the conception of post-Soviet Russia as a force that must be accommodated in order to achieve foreign policy success on the world stage. This vision has underpinned the Obama administration's unfortunate "reset" policy, which seeks to forge a new, less adversarial relationship by acknowledging—and nurturing—Russia's status as a great power.

All of this, of course, has been music to the ears of elites in Moscow, reinforcing their conception of their country's global status. Far less understood is the fact that the Russian Federation is a country fast approaching a strategic crossroads. The Kremlin now finds itself a prisoner of demographic and societal trends that will profoundly reshape the nature and workings of the Russian state.

Author and columnist Mark Steyn perhaps said it best. "What will happen in Russia?" Steyn asked wryly in the pages of *National*

Review several years ago, upon grasping the extent of the country's coming upheaval. "None of us knows, but we should know enough to know we don't know."[24]

Indeed, we do not know which direction Russia will take in the years ahead, or whether it will manage to survive at all. What is clear, however, is that Russia's future is not one of global dominance, as the current occupants of the Kremlin (and their interlocutors in the West) seem to believe. Rather, it is one of ethnic, demographic, and societal turmoil—and, quite possibly, the end of the Russia that we know.

NOTES

CHAPTER ONE

1. See, for example, Louis Charbonneau, "Russian Arms Shipment En Route to Syria: Report," Reuters, May 25, 2012, http://articles.chicagotribune.com/2012-05-25/news/sns-rt-us-syria-arms-russiabre84p00b-20120525_1_syrian-president-bashar-al-assad-cargo-ship-russian-firm.

2. For a good overview, see George L. Simpson Jr., "Russian and Chinese Support for Tehran," *Middle East Quarterly* XVII, no. 2 (Spring 2010): 63–72.

3. Keith C. Smith, "A Bear at the Door," *Journal of International Security Affairs*, no. 13 (Fall 2007): http://www.securityaffairs.org/issues/2007/13/smith.php.

4. See, for example, Ilan Berman, "Russia Shows the US the Central Asia Door," *Jane's Defence Weekly*, July 11, 2007, http://www.ilanberman.com/5923/russia-shows-the-us-the-central-asia-door.

5. Paul Klebnikov, "Gangster-Free Capitalism?" *Forbes*, November 26, 2001, http://www.forbes.com/forbes/2001/1126/107.html.

6. CSIS Global Organized Crime Project, *Russian Organized Crime* (Washington, D.C.: Center for Strategic & International Studies, 1997).

7. See, for example, Oleg Bukharin and William Potter, "Potatoes Were Guarded Better," *The Bulletin of the Atomic Scientists*, May 1995, http://books.google. com/books?id=PgwAAAAAMBAJ&pg=PA46&lpg=PA46&dq=potatoes+we re+guarded+better&source=bl&ots=2QAjY7_Ru4&sig=lwOPzIX54pA4Cx nRzn0f1vt0C2Y&hl=en&sa=X&ei=1WpPUfuYD5T_qQHQp4GwCw&ved =0CDkQ6AEwAQ#v=onepage&q=potatoes%20were%20guarded%20 better&f=false.

8. See "Pravila Dvizheniya [Rules of the Road]," *Rossiiskaya Gazeta*, no. 5804, June 9, 2012, http://www.rg.ru/2012/06/09/miting.html.

9. Brad Thayer and Thomas Skypek, "The Perilous Future of U.S. Strategic Forces," *Journal of International Security Affairs,* no. 16 (Spring 2009), http:// www.securityaffairs.org/issues/2009/16/thayer&skypek.php; Mark Schneider, "New *START*'s Dangerous Legacy," AFPC *Defense Dossier,* no. 1 (December 2011): http://www.afpc.org/files/december2011.pdf.

10. Ibid.; author's interviews, Moscow, Russia, March 2013.

11. David E. Sanger, "Obama to Renew Drive for Cuts in Nuclear Arms," *New York Times*, February 10, 2013, http://www.nytimes.com/2013/02/11/us/ politics/obama-to-renew-drive-for-cuts-in-nuclear-arms.html?_r=0.

12. "Putin: Soviet Collapse A 'Genuine Tragedy,'" Associated Press, April 25, 2005, http://www.msnbc.msn.com/id/7632057/ns/world_news/t/putin-soviet-collapse-genuine-tragedy/#.UGZYqqPaKSo.

13. Thomas de Waal et al., "The Stalin Puzzle: Deciphering Post-Soviet Public Opinion," Carnegie Endowment for International Peace, March 1, 2013, http://www.carnegieendowment.org/2013/03/01/stalin-puzzle-deciphering-post-soviet-public-opinion/fmz8#.

14. In the words of former Russian Duma Deputy Sergei Kovalev, *derzhavnost* is a neo-Soviet ideology in which the state "is deified, placed above society, outside society, over society." Sergei Kovalev, "On The New Russia," *New York Review of Books*, April 18, 1996, http://www.nybooks.com/articles/ archives/1996/apr/18/on-the-new-russia/?pagination=false.

15. See, for example, Bill Gertz, "The Bear At The Door," *Washington Free Beacon*, June 26, 2012, http://freebeacon.com/the-bear-at-the-door/; Bill Gertz,

"Putin's July 4th Message," *Washington Free Beacon*, July 6, 2012, http://freebeacon.com/putins-july-4th-message/.

16. See estimates included in Graeme P. Herd and Gagik Sargsyan, "Debating Russian Demographic Security: Current Trends and Future Trajectories," PIR Center *Security Index*, no. 83 (September 2007): http://www.pircenter.org/media/content/files/0/13412429941.pdf.

17. Nicholas Eberstadt, "The Emptying of Russia," *Washington Post*, February 13, 2004, A27.

18. Jonah Hull, "Russia Sees Muslim Population Boom," *Al-Jazeera* (Doha), January 13, 2007, http://english.aljazeera.net/news/europe/2007/01/2008525144630794963.html; "Cherez polveka Musulmani v Rossii Mogut Stat Bolshenstvom—Posol MID RF [In Half a Century, Muslims in Russia Could Become the Majority—Russia's OIC Ambassador]," Interfax (Moscow), October 10, 2007, http://www.interfax-religion.ru/islam/print.php?act=news&id=20767.

CHAPTER TWO

1. Fred Weir, "Putin Vows to Halt Russia's Population Plunge With Babies, Immigrants," *Christian Science Monitor*, February 14, 2012, http://www.csmonitor.com/World/2012/0214/Putin-vows-to-halt-Russia-s-population-plunge-with-babies-immigrants.

2. "Country Comparison: Total Fertility Rate," Central Intelligence Agency *World Factbook*, https://www.cia.gov/library/publications/the-world-factbook/rankorder/2127rank.html.

3. Ibid.

4. Ibid.

5. Mark Steyn, *America Alone: The End of the World as We Know It* (Washington, D.C.: Regnery, 2007), xv.

6. Statistics compiled from United States Census Bureau, "International Data Base," http://www.census.gov/population/international/data/idb/region.php.

7. "Country Comparison: Total Fertility Rate."

8. Charles Clover, "Putin Hails Russian Birth-Rate Bounce," *Financial Times*, December 21, 2012, http://www.ft.com/intl/cms/s/0/d65c12c4-4b71-11e2-88b5-00144feab49a.html#axzz2FHNUMdP1.

9.   Paul Goble, "Russia's Population Stabilization Only Temporary, Demographer
     Says," *Window on Eurasia*, January 19, 2010, http://windowoneurasia.
     blogspot.com/2010/01/window-on-eurasia-russias-population.html.

10. Isabel Gorst, "Russia: Love Is Not All You Need," *Financial Times Beyond
     BRICs*, August 2, 2012, http://blogs.ft.com/beyond-brics/2012/08/02/russia-
     love-is-not-all-you-need/#axzz22D4toNSs.

11. Stephan Sievert, Sergey Zakharov, and Reiner Klingholz, *The Waning World
     Power: The Demographic Future of Russia and the Other Soviet Successor
     States* (Berlin Institute for Population and Development, April 2011), http://
     www.berlin-institut.org/publications/studies/the-waning-world-power.html.

12. As recounted in Venyamin A. Baslachev, *Demografiya: Russkie Proriv.
     Nezavisimoye Isledovanie* (Demography: The Russian chasm; An independent
     investigation) (Moscow: Beluy Albii, 2006), 6.

13. Vserosiiskii Perepis Naselenie 2010, http://www.perepis-2010.ru/.

14. Vladimir Putin, "Building Justice: A Social Policy for Russia," RT.com,
     February 13, 2012, http://rt.com/politics/official-word/putin-building-justice-
     russia-133/.

15. Ibid.

16. Ibid.

17. Grace Wong, "Russia's Bleak Picture of Health," CNN, May 19, 2009, http://
     edition.cnn.com/2009/HEALTH/05/19/russia.health/index.html; see also Luke
     Harding, "No Country for Old Men," *Guardian*, February 10, 2008, http://
     www.guardian.co.uk/world/2008/feb/11/russia.

18. "List of Countries by Life Expectancy," *Wikipedia*, http://en.wikipedia.org/
     wiki/List_of_countries_by_life_expectancy.

19. Ben W. Heineman, Jr., "In Russia, A Demographic Crisis and Worries for
     Nation's Future," *Atlantic*, October 11, 2011, http://www.theatlantic.com/
     international/archive/2011/10/in-russia-a-demographic-crisis-and-worries-for-
     nations-future/246277/.

20. Statistics compiled from the World Life Expectancy website, http://www.
     worldlifeexpectancy.com/.

21. Nicholas Eberstadt and Apoorva Shah, "Russia's Great Leap Downward,"
     Journal of International Security Affairs, no. 17 (Fall 2009): 77.

22. Christopher True, "'Ghost Villages' Haunt Russian Vote," *Al Jazeera* (Doha), March 2, 2012, http://www.aljazeera.com/indepth/spotlight/russianelections/2012/03/20123272311679897.html.

23. Ibid.

24. William Moskoff, "Divorce in the USSR," *Journal of Marriage and Family* 45, no. 2 (May 1983): 419.

25. Ibid.

26. "Pervuye v Mire: Vimiraya, Razvodim Krabov" (First in the World: Dying Out, Divorce and Crabs), miloserdie.ru, http://www.miloserdie.ru/index.php?ss=20&s=36&id=17477.

27. V. I. Sakevich and B. P. Denisov, "The Future of Abortions in Russia," Paper presented to EPC-2008, Barcelona, Spain, 2008, http://epc2008.princeton.edu/papers/80419.

28. Ibid.

29. World Health Organization, "Facts and Figures About Abortion in the European Region," http://www.euro.who.int/en/what-we-do/health-topics/Life-stages/sexual-and-reproductive-health/activities/abortion/facts-and-figures-about-abortion-in-the-european-region.

30. "Pervuye v Mire: Vimiraya, Razvodim Krabov" (First in the World: Dying Out, Divorce and Crabs).

31. "Up To 2.5 Million Abortions Conducted in Russia Each Year," Interfax, January 25, 2012, http://www.interfax-religion.com/?act=news&div=9004.

32. Sarah Mendelson, "The Security Implications of HIV/AIDS in Russia," PONARS *Policy Memo*, no. 245 (February 2002): 2, http://www.gwu.edu/~ieresgwu/assets/docs/ponars/pm_0245.pdf.

33. Guy Faulconbridge, "Russia Warns Of AIDS Epidemic, 1.3 Mln With HIV," Reuters, May 15, 2007, http://www.reuters.com/article/2007/05/15/us-russia-aids-idUSL1546187520070515.

34. Ibid.

35. Mansur Mirovalev, "Russian Drug Abuse Top Problem, According to Poll," Associated Press, July 12, 2012, http://www.huffingtonpost.com/2012/07/12/russia-drug-abuse_n_1667786.html.

36. Victoria MacDonald, "Russia Condemned for Its Futile Fight against AIDS," News 4, July 19, 2012, http://www.channel4.com/news/russia-condemned-for-its-futile-fight-against-aids.

37. Simeon Bennett, "AIDS Deaths Surge in Russia and Ukraine, Defying Global Trend," Bloomberg, November 21, 2011, http://www.bloomberg.com/news/2011-11-21/aids-deaths-surge-in-russia-and-ukraine-defying-global-trend.html.

38. Adam Taylor, "AIDS-Related Deaths Are Falling Everywhere In The World—But Not Here," *Business Insider*, November 21, 2011, http://articles.businessinsider.com/2011-11-21/europe/30424547_1_unaids-report-aids-related-deaths-aids-epidemic.

39. Sergei L. Loiko, "Russians are Leaving the Country in Droves," *Los Angeles Times*, November 14, 2011, http://articles.latimes.com/2011/nov/14/world/la-fg-russia-emigration-20111115.

40. As cited in "The Mood of Russia: Time To Shove Off," *Economist*, September 13, 2011.

41. Dmitry Oreshkin, "Beg (Flight)," *Novaya Gazeta*, no. 10 (January 31, 2011): http://www.novayagazeta.ru/society/7330.html.

42. Corey Flintoff, "Educated Russians Often Lured To Leave," NPR, September 5, 2012, http://www.npr.org/2012/09/04/160548566/educated-russians-often-lured-to-leave.

43. "Kazhdiy Pyatiy Rossiyanin Hotel By Zhite Za Grantsey, Pokozal Opros (Every Fifth Russian Citizen Would Like To Live Abroad, Survey Finds)," RIA Novosti, August 6, 2012, http://ria.ru/society/20120608/668904615.html.

44. Sergei L. Loiko, "Russians Are Leaving the Country in Droves," *Los Angeles Times*, November 14, 2011, http://articles.latimes.com/2011/nov/14/world/la-fg-russia-emigration-20111115.

45. Anya Fedorova, Neil Harvey, and Lindsay France, "Russia Will Plug Brain Drain with Foreign Labor By 2030—Report," *Russia Today*, July 14, 2012, http://rt.com/news/prime-time/russia-foreign-force-hays-report-163/.

46. "MVF: Pensionniy Vozrast V Rossii Nado Uvelichet Do 63 Let (IMF: Retirement Age In Russia Should Be Raised To 63)," *Vesti*, June 13, 2012, http://www.vesti.ru/doc.html?id=819920.

47. True, "'Ghost Villages' Haunt Russian Vote," *Al-Jazeera* (Doha), March 2, 2012, http://www.aljazeera.com/indepth/spotlight/russianelections/2012/03/20123272311679897.html.

48. "Divorce-Prone Russia Marks Family Day," RIA Novosti (Moscow), July 8, 2011, http://en.rian.ru/russia/20110708/165084698.html.

49. True, "'Ghost Villages' Haunt Russian Vote," *Al-Jazeera* (Doha), March 2, 2012, http://www.aljazeera.com/indepth/spotlight/russianelections/2012/03/20123272311679897.html.

50. Hillary White, "Russia Considering Abortion Restrictions to Slow Population Collapse," Lifesitenews.com, April 28, 2011, http://www.lifesitenews.com/news/russia-considering-abortion-restrictions-to-slow-population-collapse/.

51. Sophia Kishkovsky, "Russia Enacts Law Opposing Abortion," *New York Times*, July 15, 2011, http://www.nytimes.com/2011/07/15/world/europe/15iht-russia15.html.

52. True, "'Ghost Villages' Haunt Russian Vote," *Al-Jazeera* (Doha), March 2, 2012, http://www.aljazeera.com/indepth/spotlight/russianelections/2012/03/20123272311679897.html.

53. Lena Smirnova, "Boyz II Men Expect Muscovites to Bring 'A-Game' to Concert," *Moscow Times*, January 30, 2013, http://www.themoscowtimes.com/arts_n_ideas/article/boyz-ii-men-expect-muscovites-to-bring-a-game-to-concert/474719.html.

54. As outlined in World Health Organization, *Health Systems in Transition* 13, no. 7 (2011): http://www.euro.who.int/__data/assets/pdf_file/0006/157092/HiT-Russia_EN_web-with-links.pdf.

55. "Russian Official Warns of Insufficient Spending on Education, Health, Science," Interfax, September 4, 2012 (via BBC monitoring).

56. Mark Schneider, "New START's Dangerous Legacy," American Foreign Policy Council *Defense Dossier*, no. 1 (December 2011): http://www.afpc.org/files/december2011.pdf.

57. As cited in "The Mood of Russia: Time to Shove Off," *Economist*, September 13, 2011.

58. Howard Amos, "800,000 Russians Committed Suicide Since Soviet Union Collapsed," *Telegraph*, October 21, 2011.

CHAPTER THREE

1. "Russia's Turning Muslim, Says Mufti," *Australian*, August 6, 2005, http://www.theaustralian.com.au/common/story_page/0,5744,16167042%5E2702,00.html.

2.   Statistics derived from the 2002 All Russia Population Census, *Vserossiyskaya Perepis Naseleniya 2002a Goda*, www.perepis2002.ru.

3.   "Russia's Turning Muslim, Says Mufti," *Australian*, August 6, 2005, http://www.theaustralian.com.au/common/story_page/0,5744,16167042% 5E2702,00.html.

4.   See Daniel Pipes, "The Problem of Soviet Muslims," *Asian Outlook* (Taipei), March–April 1991, http://www.danielpipes.org/206/the-problem-of-soviet-muslims.

5.   See, for example, Robert Conquest, *The Nation Killers: The Soviet Deportation of Nationalities* (London: Macmillan, 1970).

6.   See Jonah Hull, "Russia Sees Muslim Population Boom," *Al-Jazeera* (Doha), January 13, 2007, http://english.aljazeera.net/news/europe/2007/01/2008525144630794963.html.

7.   Statistics derived from the 2002 All Russia Population Census, *Vserossiyskaya Perepis Naseleniya 2002a Goda*, www.perepis2002.ru.

8.   Ibid.

9.   Pew Forum on Religion and Public Life, "The Future of the Global Muslim Population: Projections for 2010–2030," January 27, 2011, http://www.pewforum.org/future-of-the-global-muslim-population-russia.aspx.

10. "Muslim Birthrate Worries Russia," *Washington Times*, November 20, 2006, http://www.washingtontimes.com/news/2006/nov/20/20061120-115904-9135r/?page=all.

11. Judyth Twigg, "Differential Demographics: Russia's Muslim and Slavic Populations," Center for Strategic and International Studies *PONARS Policy Memo*, no. 388, December 2005, http://csis.org/files/media/csis/pubs/pm_0388.pdf.

12. Pew Forum, "The Future of the Global Muslim Population."

13. "Russian Muslim Leader Calls for Crescent as Part of National Emblem," RIA Novosti, April 15, 2011, http://en.rian.ru/russia/20110415/163540921.html.

14. Stephan Sievert, Sergey Zakharov, and Reiner Klingholz, "The Waning World Power: The Demographic Future of Russia and the Other Soviet Successor States," Berlin Institute for Population and Development, April 2011, http://www.berlin-institut.org/publications/studies/the-waning-world-power.html.

15. Ibid.

16. Ibid.

17. Jeremy Page, "The Rise of Russian Muslims Worries Orthodox Church," *Times of London*, http://www.islamawareness.net/Europe/Russia/rise.html.

18. Pipes, "Predicting a Majority-Muslim Russia," *Lion's Den* (blog), danielpipes. org, August 6, 2005, http://www.danielpipes.org/blog/2005/08/predicting-a-majority-muslim-russia.

19. Paul Goble, Remarks before the Commission on Security and Cooperation in Europe, December 17, 2009, http://csce.gov/index.cfm?FuseAction= ContentRecords.ViewTranscript&ContentRecord_id=465&ContentType=H ,B&ContentRecordType=B&CFID=25941239&CFTOKEN=36947033.

20. Michael Mainville, "Islam Thrives as Russia's Population Falls," *Toronto Star*, December 3, 2006, http://www.imra.org.il/story.php3?id=31875.

21. Ibid.

22. Hull, "Russia Sees Muslim Population Boom," *Al-Jazeera* (Doha), January 13, 2007, http://english.aljazeera.net/news/europe/2007/01/2008525144 630794963.html.

23. "Cherez polveka Musulmani v Rossii Mogut Stat Bolshenstvom—Posol MID RF [In Half a Century, Muslims in Russia Could Become the Majority— Russia's OIC Ambassador]," Interfax (Moscow), October 10, 2007, http:// www.interfax-religion.ru/islam/print.php?act=news&id=20767.

24. "Analyst Predicts Muslim Majority in Russia within 30 Years," *Voice of America*, October 31, 2009, http://www.voanews.com/content/ a-13-2006-02-28-voa77/399222.html.

25. Gordon Hahn, *Russia's Islamic Threat* (New Haven: Yale University Press, 2007), 6.

26. "The Strategy of Socio-Economic Development of the North Caucasus Federal District Until 2025," *Vestnik Kavkaza*, October 7, 2010, http://vestnikkavkaza. net/analysis/society/6671.html.

27. "Russia's Economy," *Economist*, December 22, 2011, http://www.economist. com/blogs/graphicdetail/2011/12/focus-1.

28. Sievert, Sergey Zakharov, and Reiner Klingholz, "The Waning World Power: The Demographic Future of Russia and the Other Soviet Successor States," Berlin Institute for Population and Development, April 2011, http://www. berlin-institut.org/publications/studies/the-waning-world-power.html.

29.   "Nine Tenths Of Chechens Living in Poverty: Minister," Agence France-Presse, August 18, 2005, http://reliefweb.int/report/russian-federation/russian-fed-nine-tenths-chechens-living-poverty-minister.

30.   Jacey Fortin, "For Russian-Controlled Chechnya, a Sparkling City and a Dancing Dictator," *International Business Times*, September 20, 2012, http://www.ibtimes.com/russian-controlled-chechnya-sparkling-city-dancing-dictator-793810.

31.   Sievert, Sergey Zakharov, and Reiner Klingholz, "The Waning World Power: The Demographic Future of Russia and the Other Soviet Successor States," Berlin Institute for Population and Development, April 2011, http://www.berlin-institut.org/publications/studies/the-waning-world-power.html.

32.   Jeronim Perovic, *The North Caucasus on the Brink* (Zurich: Center for Security Studies, 2006), 19, http://kms2.isn.ethz.ch/serviceengine/Files/EINIRAS/22365/ipublicationdocument_singledocument/B5E9E0D0-8C98-4C41-8F21-78FBE60063B8/en/casestudy_north_caucasus.pdf/.

33.   "Federal Subjects of Russia by Unemployment Rate," *Wikipedia*, http://en.wikipedia.org/wiki/Federal_subjects_of_Russia_by_Unemployment_Rate.

34.   "Russia's Regions: Facts and Figures," United Nations Development Programme, http://www.undp.ru/index.phtml?iso=RU&lid=1&pid=1&cmd=text&id=187.

35.   Twigg, "Differential Demographics: Russia's Muslim and Slavic Populations," Center for Strategic & International Studies *PONARS Policy Memo*, no. 388 (December 2005): http://csis.org/files/media/csis/pubs/pm_0388.pdf.

36.   Khristina Narizhnaya, "Russia's Xenophobia Problem," *GlobalPost*, April 29, 2012, http://www.globalpost.com/dispatch/news/regions/europe/russia/120427/russia-xenophobia-racism-putin-immigration-reform.

37.   Ibid.

38.   "Russians Favor Immigration Restrictions—Poll," Interfax, December 14, 2012, http://russialist.org/russians-favor-immigration-restrictions-poll/.

39.   "Racist Attacks Wound 200 People, Including 18 Lethally, in Russia in 2012—Rights Activists," Interfax, December 29, 2012, http://rbth.ru/articles/2012/12/29/racist_attacks_wound_200_people_including_18_lethally_in_russia_in_2_21605.html.

40.   Narizhnaya, "Russia's Xenophobia Problem," *GlobalPost*, April 29, 2012, http://www.globalpost.com/dispatch/news/regions/europe/russia/120427/russia-xenophobia-racism-putin-immigration-reform.

41. Alexander Verkhovsky, "The Ultra-Right in Russia in 2012," SOVA Center *Report*, December 2012, http://www.sova-center.ru/en/xenophobia/reports-analyses/2012/10/d25539/.

42. Ibid.

43. Charles Clover, "'Managed Nationalism' Turns Nasty for Putin," *Financial Times*, December 23, 2010, http://www.ft.com/intl/cms/s/0/046a3e30-0ec9-11e0-9ec3-00144feabdc0.html#axzz2KtFLqYoI.

44. Owen Matthews and Anna Nemtsova, "Fascist Russia?" *Newsweek*, August 7, 2011, http://www.thedailybeast.com/newsweek/2011/08/07/why-the-kremlin-aids-the-rise-of-russia-s-far-right-hate-groups.html.

45. Civic Chamber of the Russian Federation, *Doklad o Sostoyanii Grazhdanskovo Obshestva v Rossiyskoy Federatsii za 2012 god* [Report on the state of civil society in the Russian Federation for the year 2012] (Moscow: OPRF, 2012), 73.

46. Nadezhda Krasilova, "Moda Na Ksenophobiu [Fashion for Xenophobia]," *Noviye Izvesitiya*, February 26, 2013, http://www.newizv.ru/politics/2013-02-26/178323-moda-na-ksenofobiju.html.

47. Gordon Hahn, "The Perils of Putin's Policies," *Journal of International Security Affairs*, no. 10 (Spring 2006): http://www.securityaffairs.org/issues/2006/10/hahn.php.

48. *Presidential Decree* no. 849 (May 13, 2000), as cited in Laura Belin, "Politics and the Mass Media under Putin," in Cameron Ross, *Russian Politics under Putin* (Manchester: Manchester University Press, 2004), 158.

49. Gordon M. Hahn, "Reforming the Federation," in Stephen White, Zvi Gitelman, and Richard Sakwa, eds., *Developments in Russian Politics 6* (London: Palgrave Macmillan, 2005), 148–67.

50. Michael L. Bressler, "Politics," in Michael L. Bressler, ed., *Understanding Contemporary Russia* (Lynne Rienner Publishers, 2009), 119.

51. *Federal'nyi Zakon*, no. 168 (December 20, 2004), as cited Sarah E. Cox, "Reverse Revolution: Russia's Constitutional Crisis," Washington University *Pacific Rim Law and Policy Journal* 22, no. 1 (2013): http://digital.law.washington.edu/dspace-law/bitstream/handle/1773.1/1213/22PRLPJ179.pdf?sequence=1.

52. *Federal'nyi Zakon*, no. 107 (July 12, 2006), as cited in Cox, "Reverse Revolution."

53. Yevgeny Volk, "Russia's NGO Law: An Attack on Freedom and Civil Society," Heritage Foundation *WebMemo*, no. 1090 (May 24, 2006): http://www.heritage.org/research/reports/2006/05/russias-ngo-law-an-attack-on-freedom-and-civil-society.

54. Ibid.; Zbigniew Brzezinski, "Putin's Choice," *Washington Quarterly* 31, no. 2 (2008): 95–116.

55. Hahn, *Russia's Islamic Threat*, 19.

56. Alexei Malashenko, "The Dynamics of Russian Islam," Carnegie Moscow Center, February 1, 2013, http://carnegie.ru/2013/02/01/dynamics-of-russian-islam/f890.

57. Damir hazrat Mukhetinov, "Nabludenie Nad Tekushimi Protsesami v Rossiyskoi Musulmanskoi Obshine (Chaste 7) [Observations on the current processes in the Russian Muslim community (part 7)], November 7, 2012, http://damir-hazrat.livejournal.com/66143.html/.

58. Ibid.

CHAPTER FOUR

1. An early version of this chapter appeared in the Spring/Summer 2011 edition of the *Journal of International Security Affairs* under the title, "The Caliphate Comes Home."

2. Gordon M. Hahn, *Russia's Islamic Threat* (New Haven: Yale University Press, 2007), 31.

3. For an in-depth account of this trend, see Paul Murphy, *The Wolves of Islam: Russia and the Faces of Chechen Terror* (London: Brassey's, 2004).

4. Hahn, *Russia's Islamic Threat*, 36.

5. Ibid., 36–37.

6. Ibid., 38–39.

7. Jim Nichol, *Stability in Russia's Chechnya and Other Regions of the North Caucasus: Recent Developments* (Washington, D.C.: Congressional Research Service, January 27, 2010), 10–11, http://assets.opencrs.com/rpts/RL34613_20100127.pdf.

8. See, for example, Alexander Litvinenko and Yuri Felshtinsky, *Blowing Up Russia: The Secret Plot to Bring Back KGB Terror* (New York: Encounter Books, 2007).

9.   "Obituary: Chechen Rebel Khattab," BBC, April 26, 2002, http://news.bbc. co.uk/2/hi/europe/1952053.stm.

10. "Chechen Rebel Chief Basayev Dies," BBC, July 10, 2006, http://news.bbc. co.uk/2/hi/5165456.stm.

11. Tony Halpin, "Chechen Rebellion Has Been Crushed, Says Kremlin," *Sunday Times*, April 17, 2009, http://www.times-online.co.uk/tol/news/world/europe/ article6108444.ece.

12. "Russia," American Foreign Policy Council, *World Almanac of Islamism*, http://almanac.afpc.org/Russia.

13. Simon Shuster, "Chechen Terrorists, Despite a Schism, Come Back Ferociously," *Time*, October 21, 2010, http://www.time.com/time/world/article/ 0,8599,2026737,00.html; Charles Reckangel, "Assassination of Daghestan's Sufi Spiritual Leader Raises Specter of New Violence," *Radio Free Europe/ Radio Liberty*, December 29, 2012, http://www.rferl.org/content/daghestan- sufi-leader-suicide-bombing-/24692153.html.

14. Matthias Schepp, "Anarchy in Dagestan: Islamists Gain Upper Hand in Russian Republic," *Der Spiegel*, July 30, 2010, http://www.spiegel.de/ international/world/0,1518,709176,00.html.

15. Ibid.

16. "Sotseologi: 30 percent Molodezhi Dagestana Khotyat Zhite v Religioznom Gosudarstve [Sociologists: 30 Percent of Dagestan's Youth Wants to Live under a Religious Government]," Regnum, January 11, 2011, http://www.regnum. ru/news/polit/1363203.html.

17. Nichol, *Stability in Russia's Chechnya and Other Regions of the North Caucasus: Recent Developments* (Washington, D.C.: Congressional Research Service, January 27, 2010), 13, http://assets.opencrs.com/rpts/RL34613_20100127.pdf.

18. Author's interviews, Kazan, Russia, December 2010.

19. Rafael Khakim, *Ternistuy Put k Svobode* [The Thorny Path to Freedom] (Kazan: Tatarstan Book Press, 2007).

20. Yana Amelina, "Djihad v Tatarstane [Jihad in Tatarstan]," *Zvezda Povolzhya* (Kazan), December 2, 2010.

21. "Alleged Islamic Extremists Detained in Bashkortostan," *Radio Free Europe/ Radio Liberty*, February 8, 2011, http://www.rferl.org/content/bashkortostan_ islamists/2301430.html.

22. Hahn, *Russia's Islamic Threat* (New Haven: Yale University Press, 2007), 213–214.

23. "Hizb ut-Tahrir," American Foreign Policy Council, *World Almanac of Islamism*, July 14, 2011, http://almanac.afpc.org/hizb-ut-tahrir.

24. Shiv Malik, "The Conveyor Belt of Extremism," *New Statesman*, July 18, 2005, http://www.militantislammonitor.org/article/id/803.

25. See, for example, Ivan Gladilin, "Tatarstan Prevrashayetsa v Odnu iz Gorachikh Tochek Rossii [Tatarstan is becoming one of Russia's flashpoints]," km.ru, December 26, 2012, http://www.km.ru/v-rossii/2012/12/26/prava-i-tsennosti-russkogo-naseleniya-rossii/700628-tatarstan-prevrashchaetsya-v; see also "Russia Eliminates Terrorist Cell in West Siberia," RIA Novosti, May 14, 2010, http://en.rian.ru/russia/20100514/159013389.html.

26. Andrew Roth, "Two Muslim Officials Attacked In Southern Russia," *New York Times*, July 19, 2012, http://www.nytimes.com/2012/07/20/world/europe/two-muslim-officials-attacked-in-tatarstan-russia.html?_r=0.

27. Lyudmila Alexandrova, "Tatarstan's Mufti And His Deputy Paid A Price For Their Anti-Wahhabi Efforts," Itar-TASS, July 20, 2012, http://pda.itar-tass.com/en/c39/477517.html.

28. Ranis Islamov, "Ufa Zamedlennogo Deistviya [Ufa in Slow Motion]," *Russkiy Reportyor* (Moscow), July 26, 2010, http://www.rusrep.ru/2010/28/baskiriya/.

29. See, for example, "Alleged Islamic Extremists Detained in Bashkortostan," *Radio Free Europe/Radio Liberty*, February 8, 2011, http://www.rferl.org/content/bashkortostan_islamists/2301430.html.

30. Paul Goble, "Bashkortostan Becomes Newest Russian 'Hot Spot,'" Jamestown Foundation, *Eurasia Daily Monitor* 9, no. 225 (December 10, 2012): http://www.jamestown.org/single/?no_cache=1&tx_ttnews[swords]=8fd5893941d69d0be3f378576261ae3e&tx_ttnews[any_of_the_words]=reidar%20visser&tx_ttnews[tt_news]=40225&tx_ttnews[backPid]=7&cHash=625ca4bf7a7d3d287e33b6099bd8e165.

31. See, for example, Amelina, "Djihad v Tatarstane [Jihad in Tatarstan]," *Zvezda Povolzhya* (Kazan), December 2, 2010.

32. See, for example, "Pamfilova: Kremlin Enables 'Endemic Corruption' in North Caucasus," *The Other Russia*, April 23, 2010, http://www.theotherrussia.org/2010/04/23/pamfilova-kremlin-enables-endemic-corruption-in-north-caucasus/.

33. "Chechen Official Puts Death Toll for 2 Wars at up to 160,000," *New York Times*, August 16, 2005, http://www.nytimes.com/2005/08/15/world/europe/15iht-chech.html.

34. "Russia," American Foreign Policy Council, *World Almanac of Islamism*, http://almanac.afpc.org/Russia.

35. Alexei Malashenko, as cited in "U Nikh Tut Portreti Putina, Medvedeva, No Oni za Shariat [Here they have portraits of Putin and Medvedev, but believe in Sharia]," Slon.ru, December 3, 2009, http://slon.ru/articles/203931/.

36. Charles King and Rajan Menon, "Prisoners of the Caucasus," *Foreign Affairs*, July–August 2010, 29, 31; "Russia's Medvedev: Caucasus Corruption Threatens State," Reuters, May 19, 2010, http://www.reuters.com/article/2010/05/19/idUSLDE64I2GB; "Medvedev Advocates Tough Corruption Measures for North Caucasus," *Russia Today*, May 19, 2010, http://rt.com/politics/medvedev-measures-corruption-caucasus/.

37. "Russia's Medvedev: Caucasus Corruption Threatens State," Reuters, May 19, 2010, http://www.reuters.com/article/2010/05/19/idUSLDE64I2GB; "Medvedev Advocates Tough Corruption Measures for North Caucasus," *Russia Today*, May 19, 2010, http://rt.com/politics/medvedev-measures-corruption-caucasus/.

38. "Lider Shiitof-Azerbaijantsev v Tatarstane Poprosil u Presidenta Rossii Zashiti ot Vahhabitov [The leader of Azerbaijani Shiites in Tatarstan has asked the Russian President for Protection against Wahhabis]," Regnum, December 24, 2012, http://www.regnum.ru/news/fd-volga/tatarstan/1607876.html.

39. Gladilin, "Tatarstan Prevrashayetsa v Odnu iz Gorachikh Tochek Rossii [Tatarstan is becoming one of Russia's flashpoints]," km.ru, December 26, 2012, http://www.km.ru/v-rossii/2012/12/26/prava-i-tsennosti-russkogo-naseleniya-rossii/700628-tatarstan-prevrashchaetsya-v.

40. As cited in Hahn, *Russia's Islamic Threat* (New Haven: Yale University Press, 2007), 12.

41. "Russia," American Foreign Policy Council, *World Almanac of Islamism*, http://almanac.afpc.org/Russia.

42. Ariel Cohen, "A Threat to the West: The Rise of Islamist Insurgency in the Northern Caucasus and Russia's Inadequate Response," Heritage Foundation *Backgrounder*, no. 2643 (March 26, 2012): http://www.heritage.org/research/

reports/2012/03/a-threat-to-the-west-the-rise-of-islamist-insurgency-in-the-northern-caucasus.

43. "Ekspert: Vliyaniyu Radicalnoi Islamistskoi Ideologii, k Sozheleniu, Podverzhenuy Vse [Expert: Everyone is, unfortunately, susceptible to radical Islamist ideology]," Regnum, December 25, 2012, http://www.regnum.ru/news/fd-volga/tatarstan/1608274.html.

CHAPTER FIVE

1. As cited in Mikhail A. Alexseev, *Immigration Phobia and the Security Dilemma: Russia, Europe and the United States* (New York: Cambridge University Press, 2005), 95.

2. Siberia is made up of twelve federal subjects: the Altai Republic, Altai Krai, the Republic of Buryatia, Zabaykalsky Krai, Irkutsk Oblast, Kemerovo Oblast, Krasnoyarsk Krai, Novosibirsk Oblast, Omsk Oblast, Tomsk Oblast, the Tuva Republic, and the Republic of Khakassia. The Far East is made up of nine: Amur Oblast, the Jewish Autonomous Region, Kamchatka Krai, Magadan Oblast, Primorsky Krai, Sakha Republic, Sakhalin Oblast, Khabarovsk Krai, and Chukhotka Autonomous Okrug.

3. Herman Pirchner, *The Russian-Chinese Border: Today's Reality* (Washington, D.C.: American Foreign Policy Council, August 2002), 5.

4. "Itogi perepisi naseleniya," *Vserossiiskaya perepis' naseleniya*, http://www.perepis-2010.ru/message-rosstat.php.

5. For total number of citizens in Heilongjiang, see "Communiqué of the National Bureau of Statistics of People's Republic of China on Major Figures of the 2010 Population Census[1] (no. 2)," National Bureau of Statistics of China, April 11, 2009, http://www.stats.gov.cn/english/newsandcomingevents/t20110429_402722516.htm; for territory size, 180,000 square miles, see "Heilongjiang," China Discover, http://www.chinadiscover.net/china-tour/heilongjiangguide/heilongjiang-maps.htm.

6. Rens Lee, "The Far East between Russia, China and America," Foreign Policy Research Institute, *E-Notes*, July 2012, 1.

7. For more on the history of the Russian-Chinese Border, see Pirchner, *The Russian-Chinese Border: Today's Reality* (Washington, D.C.: American Foreign Policy Council, August 2002), 5; see also Al Santoli, *Empires of the Steppe* (Washington, D.C.: American Foreign Policy Council, 2002).

8. John Daniszewski, "Russia, China Pledge Friendship," *Los Angeles Times*, July 17, 2001, http://articles.latimes.com/2001/jul/17/news/mn-23129.
9. Mikhail Kharitinov, "'Yellow Peril' Over the Far East," *Mir Novostey* (Moscow), April 17, 2001.
10. Ibid.; "Chinese Migration Alarms Border Patrol," *Moscow Times*, July 1, 2000, http://www.themoscowtimes.com/news/article/chinese-migration-alarms-border-patrol/261282.html.
11. Pirchner, *The Russian-Chinese Border: Today's Reality* (Washington, D.C.: American Foreign Policy Council, August 2002), 8.
12. "Survey on Chinese in Far East," *People's Daily* (Beijing), January 2, 2004, http://english.peopledaily.com.cn/200401/01/eng20040101_131677.shtml.
13. Pirchner, *The Russian-Chinese Border: Today's Reality* (Washington, D.C.: American Foreign Policy Council, August 2002), 8.
14. Anatoly Medetsky, "Chinese Tourists Said To Drain Money, Resources," *Vladivostok News* (Vladivostok), July 21, 2000.
15. Pirchner, *The Russian-Chinese Border: Today's Reality* (Washington, D.C.: American Foreign Policy Council, August 2002), 8.
16. Olga Alexeeva, "Chinese Migration in the Russian Far East," *China Perspectives*, no. 3 (2008): 28, http://chinaperspectives.revues.org/pdf/4033.
17. Calculated from World Bank statistics available at http://data.worldbank.org/indicator/NY.GDP.MKTP.KD.ZG.
18. "Top Headache for China's New Leaders: Job Creation," *South China Morning Post*, November 1, 2012, http://www.scmp.com/news/china/article/1074241/top-headache-chinas-new-leaders-job-creation.
19. Maria Repnikova and Harley Balzer, "Chinese Migration to Russia: Missed Opportunities," Woodrow Wilson International Center for Scholars, *Eurasian Migration Papers*, no. 3 (2009): 11, http://www.wilsoncenter.org/sites/default/files/No3_ChineseMigtoRussia.pdf.
20. Anna Nemtsova, "Shrinking Siberia," *Newsweek*, September 17, 2012, http://www.thedailybeast.com/newsweek/2012/09/16/shrinking-siberia.html.
21. "A Bridge to Asia?" *Economist*, September 8, 2012, http://www.economist.com/node/21562240.
22. As cited in "Russia to Sell Desolate Lands to China?" Pravda (Moscow), January 30, 2012, http://english.pravda.ru/russia/economics/30-01-2012/120367-russia_far_east-0/.

23. Rachel Morarjee, "China Drives Development of Russia's Far East," *Russia Beyond the Headlines*, March 29, 2011, http://rbth.ru/articles/2011/03/29/chinese_funds_key_to_unlocking_riches_of_far_east_12642.html.
24. Ibid.
25. Pirchner, *The Russian-Chinese Border: Today's Reality* (Washington, D.C.: American Foreign Policy Council, August 2002), 5.
26. "Russia's Far East Region bans Chinese Migrant Farmers," *Want China Times*, September 26, 2012, http://www.wantchinatimes.com/news-subclass-cnt.asp x?cid=1102&MainCatID=11&id=20120926000042.
27. Bertil Lintner, "The Chinese Are Coming ... to Russia," *Asia Times*, May 27, 2006, http://www.atimes.com/atimes/Central_Asia/HE27Ag01.html.
28. Vitaly Kozyrev, "Russia's New Asia Strategy: Assessing Russia's Eastward Pivot," Center for Strategic and International Studies, November 14, 2012, http://csis.org/files/attachments/121114_rep_kozyrev_summary.pdf.
29. John Daly, "Russia's Far East—Rising Energy Superpower," oilprice.com, March 29, 2012, http://oilprice.com/Energy/Natural-Gas/Russias-Far-East-Rising-Energy-Superpower.html.
30. As cited in Segei Blagov, "Russia Mulls Far Eastern Economic Revival," Jamestown Foundation, *Eurasia Daily Monitor* 9, no. 83 (May 3, 2012), http://www.jamestown.org/single/?no_cache=1&tx_ttnews%5Btt_news%5D=39320.
31. Lee, "The Far East between Russia, China and America," Foreign Policy Research Institute, *E-Notes*, July 2012, 2.
32. Ibid.
33. Ibid., 4.
34. Alexei Arbatov, "If the West Continues the Expansion, Moscow Will Drive East," *Nezavisimaya Gazeta* (Moscow), January 3, 1997, 3.
35. "Russia's Primakov urges 'Strategic Triangle' with China, India," Agence France-Presse, December 21, 1998.
36. Jephraim P. Gundzik, "The US and that 'Other Axis,'" *Asia Times*, June 9, 2005, http://www.atimes.com/atimes/China/GF09Ad08.html.
37. "China, Russia Conduct Military Exercises," Associated Press, August 18, 2005, http://usatoday30.usatoday.com/news/world/2005-08-18-china-russia_x.htm?csp=34.

38. "UN Rejects Taiwan's Membership Bid," *China Daily*, July 24, 2007, http://www.chinadaily.com.cn/china/2007-07/24/content_5442231.htm.

39. "SCO Sends Strong Signals for West to Leave Central Asia," *People's Daily*, July 8, 2005, http://english.peopledaily.com.cn/200507/08/eng20050708_194907.html.

40. John J. Dziak, *The Military Relationship between China and Russia, 1995–2002: Russia's Role in the Development of China's Strategic Potential* (American Foreign Policy Council, 2003), 10.

41. Ibid., 5.

42. Nicklas Norling, "China and Russia: Partners with Tensions," *Policy Perspectives* 4, no. 1 (2007): http://www.silkroadstudies.org/new/docs/publications/2007/Norling_China_and_Russia.pdf.

43. "Russia And China: New Horizons for Cooperation," *Russia Today*, June 5, 2012, http://rt.com/politics/official-word/putin-russia-china-article-997/.

44. Kathrin Hille and Jamil Anderlini, "Russia and China to Strengthen Trade Ties," *Financial Times*, June 5, 2012, http://www.ft.com/intl/cms/s/0/d8999462-af27-11e1-a8a7-00144feabdc0.html#axzz2AFXROa3w.

45. Pirchner, *The Russian-Chinese Border: Today's Reality* (Washington, D.C.: American Foreign Policy Council, August 2002), 8.

46. Shoichi Itoh, *Russia Looks East: Energy Markets and Geopolitics in Northeast Asia* (Washington, D.C.: Center for Strategic & International Studies, July 2011), http://csis.org/files/publication/110721_Itoh_RussiaLooksEast_Web.pdf.

47. Karaganov, "Russia's Asian Strategy."

48. Thomas Grove, "Russian PM Warns China on Expansion; Medvedev Defends Far East," Reuters, August 9, 2012, http://www.reuters.com/article/2012/08/09/us-russia-china-territory-idUSBRE8780Y320120809.

49. Vladimir Radyuhin, "Russian Bear Wary of Chinese Dragon; Kremlin Economic Plan Warns of Chinese Threat to Country's Industries," *Straits Times* (Singapore), April 9, 2012.

50. Grove, "Russian PM Warns China on Expansion; Medvedev Defends Far East," Reuters, August 9, 2012, http://www.reuters.com/article/2012/08/09/us-russia-china-territory-idUSBRE8780Y320120809.

51. Ana Nivtova, "VOSTOK-2010—Unprecedented War Games in Full Swing in Russia's Far East," *Global Crisis News,* July 5, 2010, http://www.globalcrisisnews.com/general/vostok-2010-unprecedented-war-games-in-full-swing-in-russias-far-east-1718/.

52. Ibid.

53. "Russia Completes Restructuring Of Its Command Structure," Press Trust of India, October 23, 2010, http://brahmand.com/news/Russia-completes-restructuring-of-its-command-structure/5262/1/10.html.

54. Peter Kazimiroff, "Russia Deploys S-400 to Far East," *IHS Janes,* August 22, 2012, http://www.janes.com/products/janes/defence-security-report.aspx?id=1065970786.

CHAPTER SIX

1. "Electoralniye Presidenskiye Reitingi [Presidential electoral ratings]," Yuri Levada Analytical Center, February 26, 2013, http://www.levada.ru/26-02-2013/elektoralnye-prezidentskie-reitingi-fevral-2013.

2. "Russia Protests: Putin Opponents March in Moscow," BBC, June 12, 2012, http://www.bbc.co.uk/news/world-europe-18405306.

3. Dmitry Babich, "United Russia Fails to Win 50 Percent in State Duma Elections," *Russia Beyond The Headlines,* December 5, 2011, http://rbth.ru/articles/2011/12/05/united_russia_fails_to_win_50_percent_in_state_duma_elections_13893.html.

4. Josh Wilson, "The All-Russia People's Front: A Broad and Controversial Coalition," School of Russian and Asian Studies, June 26, 2011, http://www.sras.org/declaration_of_the_formation_of_the_all_russia_people_front.

5. A complete list of constituent organizations is available, in Russian, on the Front's official website, http://narodfront.ru/.

6. Author's conversations, Moscow, Russia, March 2013.

7. Ibid.

8. Ibid.

9. "Russia's Putin Signs NGO 'Foreign Agents' Law," Reuters, July 21, 2012, http://www.reuters.com/article/2012/07/21/us-russia-putin-ngos-idUSBRE86K05M20120721.

10. Ibid.

2

11. "Russian Authorities Raid 'Thousands' of NGOs," *Radio Free Europe/Radio Liberty*, March 22, 2013, http://www.rferl.org/content/russia-ngo-searches/24934961.html.

12. As cited in Arnaud de Borchgrave, "Testimony before the House of Representatives Committee on International Relations," October 1, 1997, http://www.russianlaw.org/Borchgrave.htm.

13. Author's conversations, Moscow, Russia, March 2013.

14. Ira Iosebashvili, "Russia's Capital Flight Intensifies," *Wall Street Journal*, January 13, 2012, http://online.wsj.com/article/SB10001424052970204409004577156242197448030.html.

15. Courtney Weaver, "Russia Makes Little Headway on Capital Flight," *Financial Times*, January 11, 2013, http://www.ft.com/intl/cms/s/0/d7bd5b1c-5c12-11e2-ab38-00144feab49a.html#axzz2OHhD0E9H.

16. Dev Kar and Sarah Freitas, *Russia: Illicit Financial Flows and the Role of the Underground Economy* (Global Financial Integrity, February 2013), http://russia.gfintegrity.org/Russia_Illicit_Financial_Flows_and_the_Role_of_the_Underground_Economy-HighRes.pdf.

17. Press Release, "Russia Hemorrhages at Least $211.5 Billion in Illicit Financial Outflows From 1994–2011—New GFI Study," Global Financial Integrity, February 13, 2013, http://www.gfintegrity.org/content/view/597/.

18. "Medvedev: Corruption 'Serious' Problem," United Press International, November 11, 2011, http://www.upi.com/Top_News/World-News/2011/11/11/Medvedev-Corruption-serious-problem/UPI-79671321034639/.

19. Masha Charney, "Dmitry Medvedev's New Assault on Corruption," *Rossiyskaya Gazeta*, April 2, 2012, http://www.telegraph.co.uk/sponsored/russianow/politics/9180719/Dmitry-Medvedev-corruption-Russia.html.

20. Matt Blake, "Was Russian Defence Minister Really Sacked Because He Was Cheating On His Wife, the Daughter of One of Putin's Closest Friends?" *Daily Mail*, November 6, 2012, http://www.dailymail.co.uk/news/article-2228701/Putin-sacks-Russian-defence-minister-Anatoly-Serdyukov-60m-corruption-scandal.html.

21. Olga Doronina, "State Duma Deputies on the Anti-Corruption Warpath," *Russia Behind the Headlines*, February 22, 2013, http://rbth.ru/politics/2013/02/22/state_duma_deputies_on_the_anti-corruption_warpath_23163.html.

22. Ibid.

23. Author's conversations, Moscow, Russia, March 2013.

24. Thomas Grove, "Church Should Have More Control over Russian Life: Putin," Reuters, February 1, 2013, http://www.reuters.com/article/2013/02/01/us-russia-putin-church-idUSBRE91016F20130201.

25. Sophia Kishkovsky, "Russian Orthodox Church Asserts Role in Civil Society," *New York Times*, December 18, 2011, http://www.nytimes.com/2011/12/19/world/europe/19iht-educLede19.html?pagewanted=all&_r=0.

26. As cited in "Know Thy Enemy: 'Church-Haters' Blacklisted," *Russia Today*, April 25, 2012, http://rt.com/politics/church-enemies-christianity-list-936/.

27. Laura Smith-Spark, "Russian Court Imprisons Pussy Riot Band Members on Hooliganism Charges," CNN, August 18, 2012, http://www.cnn.com/2012/08/17/world/europe/russia-pussy-riot-trial.

28. As cited in "Know Thy Enemy: 'Church-Haters' Blacklisted," *Russia Today*, April 25, 2012, http://rt.com/politics/church-enemies-christianity-list-936/.

29. Eric Hoffer, *The True Believer: Thoughts on the Nature Of Mass Movements* (New York: Harper Perennial Modern Classics, 2002), 17.

30. Janusz Bugajski, *Dismantling the West: Russia's Atlantic Agenda* (Washington, D.C.: Potomac Books, 2009), 121.

31. Stephen Blank, "Russia's Energy Weapon and European Security," paper presented to the conference on "NATO One Year after Georgia: National Perspectives," Washington, D.C., October 8, 2009, http://www.acus.org/files/StephenBlank-RussiaEnergy.pdf.

32. Jeff M. Smith, "The Great Game, Round Three," *Journal of International Security Affairs*, no. 17 (Fall 2009): http://www.securityaffairs.org/issues/2009/17/smith.php.

33. U.S. Department of Energy, Energy Information Administration, "Country Analysis Brief: Russia," September 18, 2012, http://www.eia.gov/countries/analysisbriefs/Russia/russia.pdf.

34. Smith, "The Great Game, Round Three," *Journal of International Security Affairs* no. 17 (Fall 2009): http://www.securityaffairs.org/issues/2009/17/smith.php.

35. Author's interviews, Moscow, Russia, March 2013.

36. "U.S. Could Surpass Saudi Output by 2020," Associated Press, October 23, 2012, http://www.usatoday.com/story/money/business/2012/10/23/us-top-oil-producer/1652937/.

37. Between mid-2003 and mid-2004, investment experienced a dramatic reversal, changing from a net inflow of some $4.6 billion to capital flight of over $5 billion. See Carola Hoyos and Arkady Ostrovsky, "Russia Fears Dollars 13bn Capital Flight After Yukos," *Financial Times* (London), November 8, 2003; "$5.5Bln Left Russia in First Half of Year," *Moscow Times*, July 5, 2004.

38. "Russia Unable to Increase Oil Production Quickly—Gref," Interfax, June 17, 2004.

39. Author's conversations, Moscow, Russia, March 2013.

40. Gleb Bryanski, "Russia to get Stronger Nuclear Navy, Putin Says," Reuters, July 30, 2012, http://uk.reuters.com/article/2012/07/30/uk-russia-putin-navy-idUKBRE86T1D020120730.

41. "Medvedev: Arctic Resources are Key to Russia's Future," *Seattle Times*, September 18, 2008, http://seattletimes.com/html/nationworld/2008187217_russia18.html.

42. William J. Broad, "Russia's Claim under Polar Ice Irks American," *New York Times*, February 19, 2008, http://www.nytimes.com/2008/02/19/world/europe/19arctic.html?adxnnl=1&adxnnlx=1311810481-IXSrMDBjzhfGopGmYcf6tw.

43. Translated and republished in English as "DOCUMENT: Russia's New Arctic Strategy," *Journal of International Security Affairs*, no. 18 (Spring 2010): http://www.securityaffairs.org/issues/2010/18/russia%27s_new_arctic_strategy.pdf.

44. Ibid.

45. "Russia Plans Arctic Army Brigades," BBC, July 1, 2011, http://www.bbc.co.uk/news/world-europe-13997324.

46. Gleb Bryanski, "Russia to get Stronger Nuclear Navy, Putin Says," Reuters, July 30, 2012, http://uk.reuters.com/article/2012/07/30/uk-russia-putin-navy-idUKBRE86T1D020120730.

47. "Russian Navy Warplanes Start Arctic Patrols," RIA-Novosti, February 14, 2013, http://en.rian.ru/military_news/20130214/179466119.html.

48. Ibid.

49. Paul Arthur Berkman, "Preventing an Arctic Cold War," *New York Times*, March 12, 2013, http://www.nytimes.com/2013/03/13/opinion/preventing-an-arctic-cold-war.html?_r=0.

CHAPTER SEVEN

1. Sophie Lambroschini, "Russia: Putin Tells OIC That Muslims Are 'Inseparable' Part of a Multiethnic Nation," *Radio Free Europe/Radio Liberty*, October 16, 2003, http://www.rferl.org/content/article/1104687.html.

2. Ibid.

3. Rinat Mukhametov, "Russian Muslims and Foreign Policy," *Russia in Global Affairs*, October 7, 2012, http://eng.globalaffairs.ru/number/Russian-Muslims-and-Foreign-Policy-15687.

4. Ariel Cohen, "The Primakov Doctrine; Russia's Zero-Sum Game with the United States," Heritage Foundation, *FYI*, no. 167 (December 15, 1997).

5. For a comprehensive overview, see Ilan Berman, "Russia and the Mideast Vacuum," Institute for Advanced Strategic & Political Studies, *Research Papers in Strategy*, no. 12 (June 2001): http://www.israeleconomy.org/strategic/strat12.pdf.

6. Interview with Foreign Minister Yevgeny Primakov, Rossiyskaya Gazeta (Moscow), December 17, 1996.

7. "Russia supports Arafat's Attending Arab Summit," Xinhua, March 25, 2002, http://news.xinhuanet.com/english/2002-03/25/content_330926.htm.

8. "Russia, EU Urge Direct Israel-Palestinian Talks," RIA Novosti, December 22, 2012, http://en.rian.ru/russia/20121222/178327927.html.

9. Ekaterina Grigorieva and Mikhail Vinogradov, "Liderov HAMAS zhdut v Moskve [HAMAS leaders are being awaited in Moscow]," *Izvestia*, February 10, 2006, http://izvestia.ru/news/311067.

10. "Talks with Hamas spoil Russia's image," BBC World Monitoring, March 3, 2006.

11. Carrie Satterlee, "Facts on Who Benefits from Keeping Saddam Hussein in Power," Heritage Foundation, *WebMemo*, 217 (February 28, 2003): http://www.heritage.org/research/reports/2003/02/facts-on-who-benefits-from-keeping-saddam-hussein-in-power#_ftn25.

12. Stockholm International Peace Research Institute (SIPRI), "Arms Transfers to Iraq, 1981–2001," http://projects.sipri.se/armstrade/IRQ_IMPORTS_1982-2001.pdf.

13. "Baghdad Shocker bares Russia-Saddam tie," Fox News, April 14, 2003, http://www.foxnews.com/story/0,2933,84102,00.html.

14. As cited in Mark Katz, "Russia and Iran: Who Is Strong-Arming Whom?" Radio Free Europe/Radio Liberty, *Newsline* 8, no. 131 (2004).

15. Ivan Matveychuk, "Moscow-Teheran: Concurrence of Interests: The Iranian Factor and Russo-American Relations," *Voyenno-Promyshlennyy Kuryer* (Moscow), February 25, 2004.

16. Sergei Sokut, "Rossiyskiy Otvet Amerike [Russia's Answer to America]," *Nezavisimoye Voyennoye Obozreniye* (Moscow), October 5, 2001, http://nvo. ng.ru/wars/2001-10-05/1_answer.html.

17. See, for example, Kokoshin's comments on *Ekho Moskvy* (Moscow), June 3, 2003; see also Alexei Arbatov and Andrei Piontkovski, "What Does Ahmadinejad Have in Common with Gavrilo Princip: Solving the Iranian Puzzle," PIR Center *Security Index* 13, no. 1, http://pircenter.org/data/ib/ Arbatoveng.pdf.

18. "Russian Expert says Iran can make Nuclear Weapons," Reuters, April 2, 2007, http://www.reuters.com/article/idUSL0241192520070402.

19. Author's conversations, Moscow, Russia, March 2013.

20. Ibid.

21. See, for example, "Expert Sees Threat to Russia from Nuclear Iran," *Rossiyskaya Gazeta* (Moscow), August 11, 2005.

22. These countries are: Iran itself; the six countries of the Gulf Cooperation Council (Saudi Arabia, Oman, Qatar, Bahrain, Kuwait, and the United Arab Emirates); Yemen; Egypt; Tunisia; Algeria; Morocco; Jordan; and Turkey. See *Nuclear Programmes in the Middle East: In the Shadow of Iran* (London: International Institute for Strategic Studies, 2008).

23. See "Algeria Trades Gas for Russian Nuclear Energy," *World Tribune*, January 24, 2007, http://www.worldtribune.com/worldtribune/07/front2454125. 1611111113.html; see also "Jordan Negotiations Construction of Nuclear Plant," *Yediot Ahronot* (Tel Aviv), February 10, 2010, http://www.ynetnews. com/articles/0,7340,L-3847013,00.html.

24. "Report: Arms Sales to Middle East Up 38 Percent," *Voice of America*, April 27, 2009, http://www1.voanews.com/english/news/a-13-2009- 04-27-voa26-68814102.html.

25. See, for example, "Russia Seeks Mideast Arms Sales Boost," UPI, September 15, 2009, http://www.upi.com/Business_News/Security-Industry/2009/09/15/ Russia-seeks-Mideast-arms-sales-boost/UPI-89011253044464/.

26. North Atlantic Treaty Organization, "Istanbul Summit Communiqué," Istanbul, June 28, 2004, http://www.nato.int/docu/pr/2004/p04-096e.htm.

27. Talal Nizameddin, *Russia and the Middle East: Towards a New Foreign Policy* (New York: St. Martin's, 1999), 160.

28. Christopher Harmer, "Backgrounder: Russian Naval Base Tartus," Institute for the Study of War, July 31, 2012, http://www.understandingwar.org/sites/default/files/Backgrounder_Russian_NavalBaseTartus.pdf.

29. Nizameddin, *Russia and the Middle East*, 269.

30. Foreign Minister Andrei Kozyrev, as cited in Nizameddin, *Russia and the Middle East*, 163.

31. Dmitri Trenin, "Why Russia Supports Assad," *New York Times*, September 18, 2011, http://www.nytimes.com/2012/02/10/opinion/why-russia-supports-assad.html.

32. Lyudmila Alexandrova, "Russia Writes off Africa's Debts," Itar-TASS, October 18, 2012, http://www.itar-tass.com/en/c39/549344.html.

33. "Syrian Opposition Blames Russia for Suffering," *CBS News*, July 11, 2012, http://www.cbsnews.com/8301-202_162-57470245/syrian-opposition-blames-russia-for-suffering/.

34. Joe Lauria, "Russia, China Veto Syria Resolution at U.N.," *Wall Street Journal*, July 19, 2012, http://online.wsj.com/article/SB10000872396390444097904577536793560681930.html.

35. Author's conversations, Moscow, Russia, March 2013.

36. Mark N. Katz, "Russia and the Arab Spring," Middle East Institute, April 3, 2012, http://www.mei.edu/content/russia-and-arab-spring.

37. Ibid.

38. Vladislav Senkovich, "Russia and Libya: What Awaits Us in the Foreseeable Future?" Russian International Affairs Council, February 14, 2012, http://russiancouncil.ru/en/inner/?id_4=148.

39. Ibid.

40. "Russia Sells Record $15.2 Billion of Arms in 2012," RIA Novosti, January 21, 2013, http://en.rian.ru/russia/20130121/178925765.html.

41. Author's conversations, Moscow, Russia, March 2013.

42. Ibid.

43. "Spiritual Sunni Leader Calls Russia 'Enemy Number One,'" *Golos Rossii* [Voice of Russia Radio], October 18, 2012, http://english.ruvr.ru/2012_10_18/ Spiritual-Sunni-leader-calls-Russia-enemy-number-one/.

CHAPTER EIGHT

1.   U.S. Department of Defense, Office of the Secretary of Defense, *Sustaining U.S. Global Leadership: Priorities for 21st Century Defense*, January 2012, www. defense.gov/news/Defense_Strategic_Guidance.pdf.

2.   See, for example, Ilan Berman, "Assessing Iran's Asia Pivot," *STRATAGEM* 8, no. 1 (January 2013).

3.   V. A. Nikonov et al., "Tihookeanskaya Strategia Rossiyii [Russia's Pacific Strategy]," Russian National Committee Council for Security Cooperation in the Asia Pacific, July 2010, http://www.russkiymir.ru/export/sites/default/ russkiymir/ru/events/advertisement/docs/Nikonov_080710.pdf.

4.   "Toward the Great Ocean, or the New Globalization of Russia," Valdai Discussion Club *Analytical Report*, July 2012, 12, http://vid-1.rian.ru/ig/valdai/ Toward_great_ocean_eng_short.pdf.

5.   Dmitri Trenin, "The End of the EU-Russian Relationship as You Know It," Valdai Discussion Club, January 8, 2013, http://valdaiclub.com/europe/53400. html.

6.   Author's conversations, Moscow, Russia, March 2013.

7.   "Disagreement on Missile Defense may Tell on Russia-NATO Cooperation in Other Areas—Ambassador," *Golos Rosii* [Voice of Russia Radio], February 9, 2013, http://english.ruvr.ru/2013_02_09/Disagreement-on-missile-defence-may-tell-on-Russia-NATO-cooperation-in-other-areas-Ambassador/.

8.   See, for example, "Moscow Unimpressed by Changes to US Missile Defense Plans," RIA-Novosti, March 18, 2013, http://en.ria.ru/world/20130318/ 180087109.html.

9.   See, for example, Finn Maigaard, "A New Direction for EU-Russia Relations?" Foreign Policy Association, February 8, 2012, http://foreignpolicyblogs. com/2012/02/08/direction-eu-russian-relations/.

10.   "Toward the Great Ocean, or the New Globalization of Russia," Valdai Discussion Club *Analytical Report*, July 2012, 23, http://vid-1.rian.ru/ig/valdai/ Toward_great_ocean_eng_short.pdf.

11. Ibid., 26.
12. Sergei Karaganov, "Russia's Asia Strategy," *Russia in Global Affairs*, July 2, 2011, http://eng.globalaffairs.ru/pubcol/Russias-Asian-Strategy-15254.
13. Author's conversations, Moscow, Russia, March 12, 2013.
14. John K. Yi, "Russia and South Korea: Much Ado about Something," *International Policy Digest*, October 26, 2011, http://www.internationalpolicydigest.org/2011/10/26/russia-and-south-korea-much-ado-about-something/.
15. David Herszenhorn, "Russia and Japan in Agreement on Natural Gas Deal," *New York Times*, September 8, 2012, http://www.nytimes.com/2012/09/09/world/europe/russia-and-japan-move-forward-on-natural-gas-deal.html?_r=0.
16. "Myanmar's Nuclear Ambitions: Secrets Will Out," *Economist*, June 10, 2010, http://www.economist.com/node/16321694.
17. Timofei Bordachev and Oleg Barabanov, "Siberia and the Far East as a Path to Russian Modernization," Valdai Discussion Club, January 23, 2013, http://valdaiclub.com/economy/53980.html.
18. Vladimir Petrovsky, "Russia and ASEAN: 15 Years as Dialogue Partners," Valdai Discussion Club, July 20, 2011, http://valdaiclub.com/asia/28620.html.
19. Speech by Deputy Prime Minister Sergei Ivanov to the IISS Shangri-la Conference, Singapore, June 2011, www.iiss.org/conferences/the-shangri-la-dialogue/shangri-la-dialogue-2011/speeches/sixth-plenary-session/sergei-ivanov/.
20. Dmitry Gorenberg, "The Southern Kuril Islands Dispute," PONARS *Eurasia Policy Memo*, no. 226 (September 2012): http://www.gwu.edu/~ieresgwu/assets/docs/ponars/pepm_226_Gorenburg_Sept2012.pdf; see also, "INFOGRAPHIC: History of the Kuril Islands Dispute," RIA-Novosti, 2012, http://en.rian.ru/infographics/20120907/175820440.html.
21. Ibid.
22. "Russia's Kuril Islands to Become Investment Heaven," *Golos Rosii* [Voice of Russia Radio], May 12, 2012, http://english.ruvr.ru/2012_05_12/74537891/.
23. "China, Russia Call for Efforts in Asia-Pacific Security," Xinhua (Beijing), September 28, 2010, http://www.chinadaily.com.cn/china/2010-09/28/content_11361116.htm.

24. Stephen Blank, "A (Multi) Polar Bear? Russia's Bid for Influence in Asia,"
     Global Asia, June 2012, http://www.globalasia.org/V7N2_Summer_2012/
     Stephen_Blank.html.

25. "Russia-China Oil Pipeline Opens," BBC, January 1, 2011, http://www.bbc.
     co.uk/news/world-asia-pacific-12103865; "China-Russia Oil Pipeline Records
     30 Million Tonnes in Delivery," Xinhua, January 2, 2013, http://www.
     globaltimes.cn/content/753302.shtml.

26. "China Wants All Oil from Russia's ESPO Pipeline," RIA Novosti, February
     2012, http://en.rian.ru/business/20120215/171326659.html.

27. Blank, "A (Multi) Polar Bear? Russia's Bid for Influence in Asia," *Global Asia*,
     June 2012, http://www.globalasia.org/V7N2_Summer_2012/Stephen_Blank.
     html.

28. Author's conversations, Moscow, Russia, March 2013.

CHAPTER NINE

1.   "Former Finance Minister Alexei Kudrin: 'We Have to Take a Chance with
     More Democracy,'" *Der Spiegel* (Hamburg), January 23, 2013, http://www.
     spiegel.de/international/world/interview-with-putin-ally-alexei-kudrin-on-
     democracy-in-russia-a-878873.html.

2.   Alexandr Dugin, *Osnovi Geopolitiki: Geopoliticheskoyo Budushiye Rossii*
     [The Foundations of Geopolitics: Russia's Geopolitical Future] (Moscow:
     Arctogia Centr, 1999).

3.   As cited in Charles Clover, "Will the Russian Bear Roar Again?" *Financial
     Times*, December 2, 2000.

4.   Dugin, *Osnovi Geopolitiki: Geopoliticheskoyo Budushiye Rossii* [The
     Foundations of Geopolitics: Russia's Geopolitical Future] (Moscow: Arctogia
     Centr, 1999), 190.

5.   Clover, "Will the Russian Bear Roar Again?" *Financial Times*, December 2,
     2000.

6.   As cited in "USSR Reborn," *Daily Mail* (London), October 5, 2011.

7.   Dugin, *Osnovi Geopolitiki: Geopoliticheskoyo Budushiye Rossii* [The
     Foundations of Geopolitics: Russia's Geopolitical Future] (Moscow: Arctogia
     Centr, 1999), 9.

8. As cited in Herman Pirchner Jr., *Reviving Greater Russia: The Future of Russia's Borders with Belarus, Georgia, Kazakhstan, Belarus and Ukraine* (Lanham, MD: University Press of America, 2005), 3.
9. Military-Industrial Commission of the Russian Federation, "Biographia [Biography]," http://oborona.gov.ru/pages/315/.
10. "Putin picks Dmitry Rogozin, a leading nationalist, to be NATO envoy," *International Herald Tribune,* January 10, 2008, http://www.nytimes.com/2008/01/10/world/europe/10iht-russia.4.9135955.html.
11. Military-industrial commission of the Russian Federation, "Main Page," http://oborona.gov.ru/.
12. Author's interviews, Moscow, Russia, March 2013.
13. Aleksandr Solzhenitsyn, *The Russian Question* (New York: Farrar, 1995).
14. Ibid.
15. Pirchner, *Reviving Greater Russia: The Future of Russia's Borders with Belarus, Georgia, Kazakhstan, Belarus and Ukraine* (Lanham, MD: University Press of America, 2005), 3.
16. As cited in Igor Torbakov, "Russian Policymakers Air Notion of 'Liberal Empire' in Caucasus, Central Asia," *Eurasianet,* October 26, 2003, http://www.eurasianet.org/departments/insight/articles/eav102703.shtml.
17. As cited in Vadim Dubnov: "The Russia We Will Never Lose; Fighting Imaginary Separatism Is an Extremely Costly Undertaking," gazeta.ru, February 10, 2012.
18. "Russians Ponder Unification with Ukraine, Belarus," *Angus Reid Global Monitor,* October 5, 2005, http://www.angus-reid.com/polls/15267/russians_ponder_unification_with_ukraine_belarus/.
19. Ibid.
20. *On The Admission to the Russian Federation and the Formation Within the Russian Federation of a New Subject,* 2001, as translated and reprinted in Pirchner, *Reviving Greater Russia: The Future of Russia's Borders with Belarus, Georgia, Kazakhstan, Belarus and Ukraine* (Lanham, MD: University Press of America, 2005), 3.
21. Ibid.
22. Ibid.

23. Denis Trifonov, "'Ivanov Doctrine' Reflects Moscow's Growing Confidence in the CIS and Beyond," *Central Asia-Caucasus Analyst*, November 19, 2003, http://www.cacianalyst.org/?q=node/1657.

24. Then Russian president Boris Yeltsin, as cited in Helena Yakovlev Golani, "Two Decades of the Russian Federation's Foreign Policy in the Commonwealth of Independent States: The Cases of Belarus and Ukraine," Hebrew University of Jerusalem European Forum, *Working Paper*, 2011, 18, http://www.ef.huji. ac.il/publications/Yakovlev%20Golani.pdf.

25. Pirchner, *Reviving Greater Russia: The Future of Russia's Borders with Belarus, Georgia, Kazakhstan, Belarus and Ukraine* (Lanham, MD: University Press of America, 2005).

26. "Russian PM Says Unification with Belarus Possible and Desirable," *VOA News*, July 31, 2011, http://www.voanews.com/content/russian-pm-says-unification-with-belarus-possible-and-desirable—126555343/170796.html.

27. Samuel P. Huntington, *The Clash of Civilizations and the Remaking of World Order* (New York: Simon & Schuster, 1996), 164.

28. Pirchner Jr., *Reviving Greater Russia: The Future of Russia's Borders with Belarus, Georgia, Kazakhstan, Belarus and Ukraine* (Lanham, MD: University Press of America, 2005).

29. Paul Quinn-Judge and Yuri Zarakhovich, "The Orange Revolution," *Time*, November 28, 2004, http://www.time.com/time/magazine/article/0,9171,832225,00.html.

30. Rajan Menon and Alexander J. Motyl, "Counterrevolution in Kiev," *Foreign Affairs*, November–December 2011, http://www.foreignaffairs.com/articles/136408/rajan-menon-and-alexander-j-motyl/counterrevolution-in-kiev.

31. "Poll: Ukrainians Support Unification with Russia more than Russians," *Kyiv Post*, March 25, 2011, http://www.kyivpost.com/content/ukraine/poll-ukrainians-support-unification-with-russia-mo-100860.html.

32. See, for example, Elizabeth Owen, "Georgia: Moving from Revolution to Democratic Institutions," *Eurasianet*, November 27, 2005, http://www.eurasianet.org/departments/insight/articles/eav112805.shtml.

33. Charles King, "Clarity in the Caucasus?" *Foreign Affairs*, October 11, 2009, http://www.foreignaffairs.com/articles/65469/charles-king/clarity-in-the-caucasus.

34. "Q&A: Conflict in Georgia," BBC, November 11, 2008, http://news.bbc.co.uk/2/hi/europe/7549736.stm.

35. "Day-by-Day: Georgia-Russia Crisis," BBC, August 21, 2008, http://news.bbc.co.uk/2/hi/europe/7551576.stm.

36. "Medvedev submits 2010 military base agreements with S. Ossetia, Abkhazia to Duma for ratification," Interfax, August 8, 2011.

37. "Report: Russia to Build Naval Base in Rebel Region," CNN, January 26, 2009, http://articles.cnn.com/2009-01-26/world/russia.abkhazia.naval.base_1_south-ossetia-abkhazia-russian-military-bases?_s=PM:WORLD.

38. Jim Nichol, "Armenia, Azerbaijan, and Georgia: Political Developments and Implications for US Interests," Congressional Research Service, September 27, 2012, http://fpc.state.gov/documents/organization/199404.pdf.

39. "Russia Recognizes Georgia's Breakaway Republics," RIA-Novosti, August 28, 2008, http://en.rian.ru/russia/20080826/116291407.html.

40. "International Recognition of South Ossetia and Abkhazia," *Wikipedia*, http://en.wikipedia.org/wiki/International_recognition_of_Abkhazia_and_South_Ossetia.

41. Olesya Vartanyan and Ellen Barry, "Georgian Sees Closer Ties with Russia," *New York Times*, February 5, 2013, http://www.nytimes.com/2013/02/06/world/europe/georgias-ivanishvili-sees-warming-with-russia.html?_r=0.

42. Sergei Fomin, "Derussificatsiya: Nerazreshennie Vopros [De-Russification: An Unanswered Question]," *Litiraturnaya Gazeta*, no. 44 (November 7, 2012): http://www.lgz.ru/article/20184/.

CHAPTER TEN

1. Roman Muzalevsky, "NATO Supply Routes to Afghanistan under Threat," Jamestown Foundation *Eurasia Daily Monitor* 8, no. 221 (December 6, 2011): http://www.jamestown.org/single/?no_cache=1&tx_ttnews[tt_news]=38749.

2. David Satter, "The Russian Stake in Afghanistan," Foreign Policy Research Institute, *E-Notes*, March 2013, http://www.fpri.org/articles/2013/03/russian-stake-afghanistan.

3. "Russia Approves Ulyanovsk NATO Hub," RIA Novosti, June 29, 2012, http://en.ria.ru/russia/20120629/174312840.html.

4. Herman Pirchner Jr., "A False Start with Russia," *Journal of International Security Affairs*, no. 23 (Fall/Winter 2012): 89.

5. See, for example, Keith B. Payne, "Postscript on New START," *National Review*, January 18, 2011, http://www.nationalreview.com/articles/257329/postscript-new-start-keith-b-payne.

6. David M. Herszenhorn, "Progress is Reported in Arms Talks with Russia," *New York Times*, March 21, 2013, http://www.nytimes.com/2013/03/22/world/europe/us-and-russia-report-progress-on-arms-talks.html?_r=0.

7. White House, Office of the Press Secretary, "Fact Sheet on U.S. Missile Defense Policy," September 17, 2009, http://www.whitehouse.gov/the_press_office/FACT-SHEET-US-Missile-Defense-Policy-A-Phased-Adaptive-Approach-for-Missile-Defense-in-Europe.

8. "Obama Tells Russia's Medvedev More Flexibility after Election," Reuters, March 26, 2012, http://www.reuters.com/article/2012/03/26/us-nuclear-summit-obama-medvedev-idUSBRE82P0JI20120326.

9. See, for example, "Moscow Unimpressed by Changes to US Missile Defense Plans," RIA Novosti, March 18, 2013, http://en.ria.ru/world/20130318/180087109.html.

10. Melissa Hogenboom, "America and Russia: Uneasy Partners in Space," BBC, February 10, 2012, http://www.bbc.co.uk/news/science-environment-17074388.

11. "Medvedev Prolongs Russia-US Agreements on Cooperation in Space Research until 2020," *Golos Rosii* [The Voice of Russia Radio], March 23, 2013, http://english.ruvr.ru/2013_03_23/Medvedev-prolongs-Russia-US-agreements-on-cooperation-in-space-research-until-2020/.

12. Pirchner, "A False Start with Russia," *Journal of International Security Affairs*, no. 23 (Fall/Winter 2012).

13. As cited in "Putin Outlines Pragmatic Diplomacy in Marathon News Conference," Xinhua (Beijing), December 20, 2012, http://english.sina.com/world/2012/1220/540224.html.

14. Pirchner Jr., "A False Start with Russia," *Journal of International Security Affairs*, no. 23 (Fall/Winter 2012).

15. Kathy Land and Will Englund, "Russia Fumes as U.S. Senate Passes Magnitsky Law Aimed at Human Rights," *Washington Post*, December 6, 2012, http://www.washingtonpost.com/world/europe/us-passes-magnitsky-bill-aimed-at-russia/2012/12/06/262a5bba-3fd5-11e2-bca3-aadc9b7e29c5_story.html.

16.   Office of the President of Russia, "A Law on Sanctions for Individuals Violating Fundamental Human Rights and Freedoms of Russian Citizens has been Signed," December 28, 2012, http://eng.kremlin.ru/acts/4810.

17.   Leon Aron, "The Putin Doctrine," *Foreign Affairs*, March 8, 2013, http://www.foreignaffairs.com/articles/139049/leon-aron/the-putin-doctrine?page=show.

18.   Ibid.

19.   Author's conversations, Moscow, Russia, March 2013.

20.   John Arquilla, "Civil Savant," *Foreign Policy*, January 7, 2013, http://www.foreignpolicy.com/articles/2013/01/07/civil_savant; see also John Schutte, "Casting Net Assessment: Andrew W. Marshall and the Epistemic Community of the Cold War," unpublished thesis, Air University School of Advanced Air and Space Studies, June 2012.

21.   Author's conversations, Moscow, Russia, March 2013.

22.   Aleksandr Solzhenitsyn, *The Russian Question* (New York: Farrar, 1995).

23.   Author's conversations, Moscow, Russia, March 2013.

24.   Mark Steyn, "The Bear Goes Walkabout," *National Review*, December 16, 2006, http://www.freerepublic.com/focus/f-news/1781695/posts.

ACKNOWLEDGMENTS

When I began my career in foreign policy nearly a decade and a half ago, I was supposed to do so as a Russia "hand." I had focused on Middle Eastern affairs in college and immersed myself in the study of terrorism and radical Islam in graduate school. But I was also the child of Soviet *refuseniks* and a native Russian speaker. So when, after a brief stint in the counterterrorism field, I was hired away by the American Foreign Policy Council (AFPC) to head up its analytical work on Russia, it seemed like a logical move.

That was shortly before September 11, 2001, and life quickly intervened. More than a dozen years of work on the Middle East, radical Islam, and Iran followed, spawning countless articles, op-eds, and media appearances, as well as two books on Mideast affairs (*Tehran Rising*, published in 2005, and subsequently 2009's *Winning The Long War*). But Russia has never been far from my thoughts, for both personal and practical reasons. With this book, I finally have the chance to turn to the subject in earnest.

That I have been able to do so is a credit to AFPC president Herman Pirchner, who has served as my mentor for more than a decade. Time and again, he has tirelessly encouraged my curiosity about the Russian state and its geopolitical direction. And in his own understated way, Herman has been instrumental in nudging this project along (including by scheduling a fact-finding mission to Russia's Volga region in the dead of winter several years ago). For all that, and for his continued friendship, I am tremendously grateful.

But this work quite simply would not have been possible without the assistance of a cadre of talented young scholars, all of whom lent their considerable research skills to the cause. Margot Van Loon, Heather Stetten, Cory Bender, Caitlyn McAllister, Lisa Aronson, Isaac Medina, and a host of others helped me extensively in compiling, and then deciphering, veritable mountains of data relating to Russian foreign policy and domestic trends. To the extent that this volume breaks new ground, they deserve the lion's share of the credit. Any errors that this book may contain, however, are mine and mine alone.

Thanks also go to my colleagues at AFPC—Rich Harrison, Jeff Smith, Annie Swingen, and Cheri Ady—for their friendship, and for making every day at the office an adventure. Liz Wood, AFPC's in-house editor, deserves gratitude as well for helping to refine my writing and polish my language, as she has on so many other occasions. The final product also benefited enormously from the insights of several Russia experts, including Gordon Hahn, Stephen Blank, and Wayne Merry, who lent their eyes, ears, and expertise to making sure that I got both the style and the substance of this work right.

Most of all, I owe an enormous debt of gratitude to my wonderful wife, Hillary, and to my beautiful children, Mark and Lauren. Their patience, love, and support sustained me through this project, as it always does. I hope that this book gives them a better understanding of the country our family once called home, and what the future could hold in store for it.

—Ilan Berman
Washington, D.C.
April 2013

APPENDIX ONE

THE FOUNDATIONS OF RUSSIAN FEDERATION POLICY IN THE ARCTIC UNTIL 2020 AND BEYOND

ISSUED SEPTEMBER 18, 2008*

In late March 2009, the Russian government publicly released the full text of its new Arctic strategy. That document, first issued in September 2008, lays out a dramatic expansion of official Russian sovereign interests in what was previously agreed-upon as part of the so-called "global commons." It also provides a roadmap for how Moscow will seek to rewrite the regional legal and political order in the years ahead. The translation has been reproduced below.

I. GENERAL PROVISIONS

1. Current principles determine the main goals, main challenges, strategic priorities, and mechanisms for implementing the state policy of the Russian Federation in the Arctic, as well as the means for strategic planning of the socioeconomic development of Russian Federation's Arctic zone and the maintenance of national security of the Russian Federation.

---

* Translated from the Russian by Maxim Rusnak and Ilan Berman.

2. Based on current principles, the Arctic zone of the Russian Federation is understood as the part of the Arctic which includes, either fully or partially, the territories of the Republic of Saha (Yakutiya), Murmansk and Arkhangelsk regions, Krasnoyarsk Krai, Nenets, Yamalo-Nenets, and Chukotka Autonomous Okrug, as defined by the decision of the Government Commission on Arctic Issues under the Council of Ministers of the U.S.S.R. on April 22, 1989, as well as landmasses and islands included in the Decision of the Presidium of the Central Executive Committee of the U.S.S.R. on April 15, 1926, in its "declaration of landmasses and islands in the Arctic Ocean as territories of the USSR," and water bodies attached to these territories, landmasses, and islands, territorial sea, exclusive economic zon,e and continental shelf of the Russian Federation, inside which Russia retains sovereign rights and jurisdiction, in accordance with international law. The borders of the Arctic zone of the Russian Federation can be defined in accordance to the normative legal acts of the Russian Federation, as well as by the norms of international contracts and agreements of which the Russian Federation is a participant.

3. The special features of the Arctic zone of the Russian Federation, which influence the formation of governmental policy in the Arctic, include the following:

a) extreme climate conditions, including constant ice cover or drifting ice masses in the Arctic seas;

b) the unique character of economic and industrial development of the territory and low population density;

c) the distance from major industrial centers, high resource capacity, and dependence of the private and public sectors on the delivery of energy and goods from other regions within Russia;

d) low levels of stability of ecological systems, which establish biological balance and climate of the Earth, and their dependence on the smallest anthropogenic effects.

II. NATIONAL INTERESTS OF THE RUSSIAN FEDERATION IN THE ARCTIC

4. The main national interests of the Russian Federation in the Arctic are:

a) the utilization of the Russian Federation's Arctic zone as a national strategic resource base capable of fulfilling the socioeconomic tasks associated with national growth;

b) the preservation of the Arctic as a zone of peace and cooperation;

c) the protection of the Arctic's unique ecological system;

d) the use of the North Sea passage as a unified transportation link connecting Russia to the Arctic.

5.   National interests determine the main goals, main challenges and strategic priorities of Russia's governmental policy in the Arctic. The realization of the Russian Federation's national interests in the Arctic is provided for by government institutions together with institutions of the civil society in strict accordance with the law of the Russian Federation and Russia's international contracts.

III. MAIN GOALS AND STRATEGIC PRIORITIES OF RUSSIAN STATE POLICY IN THE ARCTIC

6.   The main goals of the Russian Federation's official state policy in the Arctic are:

a) in the sphere of socioeconomic development, to expand the resource base of the Arctic zone of the Russian Federation, which is capable in large part of fulfilling Russia's needs for hydrocarbon resources, aqueous biological resources, and other forms of strategic raw material;

b) in the sphere of national security, the protection and defense of the national boundary of the Russian Federation, which lies in the Arctic zone of the Russian Federation, and the provision of a favorable operating environment in the Arctic zone for the Russian Federation, including the preservation of a basic fighting capability of general purpose units of the Armed Forces of the Russian Federation, as well as other troops and military formations in that region;

c) in the sphere of ecological protection, the preservation and protection of the natural ecosystem of the Arctic, and the mitigation of the ecological consequences of increased economic activity and global climate change;

d) in the sphere of information technology and telecommunications, the formation of a unified information space in the Arctic zone of the Russian Federation;

e) in the sphere of international cooperation, guaranteeing mutually beneficial bilateral and multilateral cooperation between the Russian Federation and other Arctic states on the basis of

international treaties and agreements to which the
Russian Federation is a signatory.

7.   The main strategic priorities of the Russian Federa-
     tion's official state policy in the Arctic are:

a) the active interaction of the Russian Federation
    with other Arctic states for the purposes of
    delineating maritime boundaries on the basis of
    international legal norms and cooperative
    agreements, taking into account the national
    interests of the Russian Federation;

b) the increase in efforts of Arctic states to create a
    unified regional system of search and rescue, as well
    as prevention of technical accidents and the
    mitigation of their consequences, including the
    coordination of rescue forces;

c) the strengthening of Russia's relations with other
    Arctic states, both bilateral and multilateral,
    including the Arctic Council and the Barents Euro-
    Arctic Region, by promoting greater economic,
    scientific, technological, and cultural interaction,
    as well as cooperation in the field of border control
    and in the areas of natural resources and ecosystem
    preservation in the Arctic;

d) assistance in the creation and use of transit and cross-polar aerial routes in the Arctic, as well as in the use of the North Sea passage for international maritime navigation within the jurisdiction of Russian Federation and in accordance to Russia's international agreements;

e) the promotion of participation of Russian state organizations and public organizations in the activities of international forums dedicated to the Arctic, including inter-parliamentary cooperation within the Russia-EU partnership;

f) the delineation of the maritime territory of the Arctic Ocean and securing a mutually beneficial presence for the Russian Federation on the Spitsbergen peninsula;

g) the improvement in state management of the socioeconomic development of the Arctic zone of the Russian Federation, including the expansion of applied scientific research in the Arctic;

h) an improvement in the quality of life of the indigenous population of the Arctic and the social conditions of economic development in the Arctic;

i) the development of the resource base of the Russian Federation's Arctic zone through the use of promising technologies;

j) the modernization and development of the transportation infrastructure and fishing industry of the Russian Federation's Arctic zone.

IV. MAIN CHALLENGES AND MEANS FOR IMPLEMENTING RUSSIAN STATE POLICY IN THE ARCTIC

8. The main goals of the state policy of the Russian Federation in the Arctic are achieved by solving the following basic problems:

a) in the area of socioeconomic development it is necessary:

—to finalize the collection of geological, geophysical, hydrographical, and cartographical data necessary for the delineation of the outer border of the Arctic zone of the Russian Federation;

—to provide for an increase in the reserves of natural resources originating in Arctic waters, partially by launching state programs for investigating and integrating the continental shelf of the Russian Federation, as well as by initiating the process of mastering the natural gas and oil reserves in the Arctic zone of the Russian Federation;

—to develop and introduce new technologies designed to acquire sea minerals and aqueous natural resources under Arctic conditions, including in ice-covered regions, and to create a base for aviation technology and fishing vessels, as well as the necessary infrastructure for work under Arctic conditions;

—to optimize the economic mechanisms of the "Northern Delivery" project, by utilizing renewable and alternative sources of energy, including local sources, and by reconstructing and modernizing energy production;

—to promote the restructuring of North Sea Passage traffic, by means of state support for the production of icebreaking, emergency, rescue and support vessels, as well as coastal infrastructure;

—to establish a system of maritime navigation security and transportation control in regions of intense naval traffic, including through the creation of a set of hydro-meteorological and navigational provisions for the Arctic zone of the Russian Federation;

—to create a system of complex security for the defense of the territories, population, and objects in the Arctic zone of the Russian Federation critically vital to Russian national security from threats of natural and technical character.

The primary means for implementing state policy in the area of socioeconomic development of the Arctic zone of the Russian Federation are:

—government support for industrial subjects active in the Arctic zone of the Russian Federation, specifically in the areas of hydrocarbon and other natural resources, by the means of utilizing innovative technology, developing transportation and energy infrastructure, improving customs and tax regulation;

—stimulating the expansion and completion of new Arctic assimilation projects by co-financing them with the aid of various levels of the Russian budget system and outside resources, and by guaranteeing state payment for labor, including research and exploration;

—modernization of social infrastructure, including educational facilities and medical facilities, as well as construction of housing and national projects of high priority;

—provision of training for specialists for work in Arctic conditions, and of assurance of government aid and compensation for persons working and living in the Arctic zone of the Russian Federation;

—provision of accessible and quality medical care for all peoples living and working in the Arctic zone of the Russian Federation, partially by expanding and modernizing first-aid systems;

—improvement of educational programs for the native population of the Arctic zone of the Russian Federation, especially by preparing children for life in a modern society with the ability to cope with extreme weather conditions, including equipping educational facilities and remote residential areas with technology necessary for distance learning;

—guaranteeing the implementation of nature preservation techniques and ecologically safe tourism in the areas of residence of native peoples, as well as the preservation of their culture, language, and tradition.

b) in the sphere of military security, defense, and protection of the Russian border in the Arctic zone of the Russian Federation it is necessary to do the following:

—to create general purpose military formations drawn from the Armed Forces of the Russian Federation, as well as other troops and military formations (most importantly, border units) in the Arctic zone of the Russian Federation, capable of ensuring security under various military and political circumstances;

—to optimize the complex system of control over
the situation in the Arctic, including border control
at the entry points to the Russian Federation, the
introduction of an administrative border regime
in the Arctic Zone, and technical control over
straits, river mouths, estuaries on the North Sea
Passage;

—improve the capabilities of the border troops to
match the sophistication of potential threats to
Russian national security in the Arctic.

The main means of implementing state policy in the area of
military security, protection of territorial integrity and border of the Russian Federation in the Arctic are the following:

—the creation of an active, functioning system of
coastal security within the Federal Security Service
(FSB) in the Arctic zone of the Russian Federation,
and an increase in the effectiveness of cooperation
with the border guard of neighboring states on the
issues of maritime terrorism, contraband, illegal
migration, and the protection of sea-based
resources;

—the development of border infrastructure along
the Arctic zone of the Russian Federation, and
re-equipment of its border guard;

—the creation of an administrative system dealing
with the maritime situation in the Arctic zone of

the Russian Federation, and strengthening of governmental control over economic activity in the Russian Arctic zone.

c) in the area of ecological security, it is necessary to do the following:

—to guarantee the preservation of biological diversity of Arctic flora and fauna, partially by expanding the network of natural preserves, in order to preserve the Arctic ecosystem in the face of expanding economic and industrial activities and climate change;

—to utilize nuclear-powered vessels during their established periods of operation.

The main means for implementing official state policy in the area of ecological security in the Arctic zone of the Russian Federation are:

—the establishment of special rules for the exploitation of natural resources and environmental protection, including the monitoring of pollution, in the Arctic zone of the Russian Federation;

—the re-cultivation of natural landscapes, the utilization of toxic waste abatement, and the establishment of biochemical safeguards, especially in densely-populated areas.

d) in the area of informational technology, it is necessary:

—to introduce modern information and telecommunication technology (including mobile) for the purposes of broadcasting, navigation (both of sea vessels and airplanes), remote sensing of the Earth, monitoring the glacial layer, as well as hydro-meteorological and hydrographic provisions and systems for scientific research;

—to create a reliable system for navigation, hydro-meteorological and informational services, guaranteeing effective control over economic, military, and ecologic activity in the Arctic, as well as predicting catastrophic situations, mitigating damage in case of their occurrence, partially by utilizing the global satellite navigation system GLONASS.

The main means for implementing official state policy in the area of information technology and communication in the Arctic zone of the Russian Federation must be directed towards production and mass usage of innovative technologies, including cosmic means and multi-process universal networks.

e) in the area of science and technology, it is necessary:

—to introduce innovative technologies, including those used for clearing the territories of islands, coastal zones, and the waters of the Arctic from anthropogenic pollution, as well as to develop materials and products suitable for the environmental conditions of the Arctic;

—to guarantee the creation of a government program for naval research, overseeing deepwater and hydronautics, to include technical instruments suitable for conducting polar research.

The main means for implementing official state policy in the area of scientific research in the Arctic zone of the Russian Federation are:

—establishing long-term perspectives and trends for various types of activity in the Arctic;

—studying dangerous and hazardous natural occurrences in the region, as well as developing and implementing innovative technologies and methods to predict the changing climate;

—forecasting and analyzing the consequences of global climate change taking place in the Arctic zone of the Russian Federation due to naturally-occurring factors, over the medium and long term, in the middle-term and long-term perspectives, including on the stability of infrastructure;

—conducting research on the history, culture, and economics of the region, as well as law enforcement activity in the Arctic;

—studying the effects of hazardous factors on the health of residents, the establishment of standards for medical care of the Arctic population, and the creation of a set of measures aimed at improving the wellbeing of the ecosystem and local residents.

9. The solution to the main tasks of official Russian state policy in the Arctic is implemented through strategic planning for the socioeconomic development of the Arctic zone of the Russian Federation, and providing for Russian national security:

   a) the development and implementation of a strategy for the Arctic zone of the Russian Federation aimed at protecting national security;

   b) the creation of a monitoring system, including through the improvement of informational and statistical observation, for tracking potential national security threats in the Arctic zone of the Russian Federation;

   c) the preparation of normative legal assessments to clarify the geographic boundaries of the Arctic zone of the Russian Federation, in particular its southern zone, along with a list and status of all local governmental bodies located within each zone;

d) an increase in the effectiveness of administration of the Arctic zone of the Russian Federation.

V. MAIN MECHANISMS FOR IMPLEMENTING OFFICIAL RUSSIAN STATE POLICY IN THE ARCTIC

10. The state policy of the Russian Federation in the Arctic is carried out by the relevant federal organs of the executive branch, governmental organs of the Russian Federation, organs of local authorities, and commercial and non-commercial organizations active within the public-private partnership framework, as well as within the framework of Russian cooperation with other states and international organizations, including:

   a) improvement, taking into consideration the national interests of Russia and the specific character of the region, of legislation in the areas of socioeconomic development, environmental protection, military security, border protection, scientific research and international cooperation in the Arctic on the basis of international legal norms and the Russian Federation's international responsibilities;

   b) development and implementation of special programs, financed by the various levels of the budgetary system of the Russian Federation and other extra-budgetary sources;

c) introduction of strategies aimed at developing territorial planning schemes and socioeconomic development programs for subjects of the Russian Federation;

d) elaboration by the means of mass media of questions dealing with the national interests of the Russian Federation in the Arctic, including organizing exhibitions, conferences, "roundtable" meetings dedicated to Russian explorers of the Arctic, all with the aim of creating a positive image of Russia;

e) organization of systematic monitoring and analysis of Russian state policy implementation in the Arctic.

VI. IMPLEMENTATION OF RUSSIAN STATE POLICY IN THE ARCTIC

11.   Current principles will be achieved in several steps:

a) during the first stage (2008–2010), the following must be accomplished:

—conducting geologic, geophysical, hydrographic, cartographic, and other research for the purpose of preparing materials for delineating the border of the Arctic zone of the Russian Federation;

—expansion of possibilities for international cooperation, partially for effective utilization of natural resources of the Arctic zone of the Russian Federation;

—realization of goal-based programs, financed by means of various budgets of the Russian Federation as well as extra-budgetary sources, including the creation of a government program dedicated to developing the Arctic zone until the year 2020, within which high-tech energy production and fishing clusters, as well as special economic zones, will be created;

—realization of promising public-private sector investment projects related to the strategic development of the Arctic zone of the Russian Federation.

b) during the second stage (2011–2015), the following must be accomplished:

—delineation of the internationally-recognized exterior border of the Arctic zone of the Russian Federation, and realization on this basis of the competitive advantages of Russia in the extraction and delivery of energy resources;

—structural reconstruction of the economy in the Arctic zone by expanding the mineral and raw-materials base and utilizing sea-based biological resources of the region;

—formation and development of infrastructure and administration systems for effective communication along the North Sea Passage and for improvement of Eurasian transit paths;

—completion of a single informational space for the Arctic zone of the Russian Federation.

c) during the third stage (2016–2020), it will be necessary to establish the Arctic zone of the Russian Federation as a leading strategic and resource base for Russia. Overall, in the mid-term, the implementation of official policy will allow the Russian Federation to maintain its status as a leading Arctic power. In the long run, it is necessary to utilize Russia's comparative advantage to strengthen its position in the Arctic, enhance international security, and maintain peace and stability in the region.

APPENDIX TWO

NATIONAL SECURITY STRATEGY
OF THE RUSSIAN FEDERATION TO 2020

Issued in May 2009 by then President Dmitry Medvedev, *Russia's National Security Strategy to 2020* lays out an exceedingly ambitious reconception of the country's strategic interests, its priorities, and its place in the world. Little attention, however, is paid to the demographic, religious, and territorial challenges now facing the Russian state.

Approved
By Decree of the President
Of the Russian Federation
May 12, 2009, no. 537

National Security Strategy of the Russian Federation to 2020*

I. GENERAL PROVISIONS

1. Russia has overcome the consequences of the systemic political and socioeconomic crisis of the end of the twentieth century—having stopped the decline in the quality of life of Russian citizens; withstood the pressures of nationalism, separatism and international

---

*Unofficial open source translation. Verified by Heather Stetten of the American Foreign Policy Council. Russian language original available at the following website, http://archive.kremlin.ru/text/docs/2009/05/216229.shtml.

terrorism; prevented the discretization of the constitutional form of government; preserved its sovereignty and territorial integrity; and restored the country's potential to enhance its competitiveness and defend its national interests as a key player within evolving multipolar international relations.

Russia is pursuing a state policy of national defense, state and social security, and stable development, which responds adequately to internal and external conditions. The preconditions for reinforcing the system of national security have been created, and the relevant legal space has been consolidated. Priority issues in the economic sphere have been resolved, and the attractiveness of the economy for investment has grown. Authentically Russian ideals and spirituality are being born, alongside a dignified attitude to historical memory. Social harmony is being formed on the basis of shared values — the freedom and independence of the Russian state, humanism, the peaceful coexistence and cultural unity of Russia's multinational population, respect for family traditions, and patriotism.

Overall, the preconditions have been formed for the reliable preemption of internal and external threats to national security, as well as for the dynamic development and transformation of Russia into a world leader with regards to the level of technological progress, quality of life, and influence over global affairs.

In the context of the globalization of processes of world development, as well as of international political and economic relations, which creates new threats and risks to the development of the individual, society, and the state, Russia is transitioning to a new state national security policy, as a guarantee of successful national development.

2. The main directions of the national security policy of the Russian Federation are the [so-called] strategic national priorities, in the form of important social, political, and economic transformations intended to create secure conditions for the realization of Russian citizens' constitutional rights and freedoms, the stable development of the country, and the preservation of the territorial integrity and sovereignty of the state.

3. The National Security Strategy of the Russian Federation until 2020 is an officially acknowledged system of strategic priorities, goals, and measures with regards to domestic and foreign policy, which determine the degree of national security and the level of stable, long-term development of the state.

Conceptual assumptions in the area of ensuring national security are based on the fundamental interconnectedness and interdependence of the National Security Strategy of the Russian Federation to 2020 and the Concept for Long-Term

SocioEconomic Development of the Russian Federation to 2020.

4.   The given Strategy forms the basis of the development of a system ensuring the national security of the Russian Federation, and presents a plan of action and measures intended to guarantee national security. It lays the foundations for constructive interaction among state bodies, organizations and social groups, in order to defend Russia's national interests and safeguard the security of the individual, society and the state.

5.   The main purpose of the given Strategy is to formulate and support, with the aid of national security forces, the internal and external conditions conducive to the implementation of strategic national priorities.

6.   The given Strategy employs the following concepts:

—"national security"—the protection of the individual, society, and the state from domestic and foreign threats, which, in turn, ensures constitutional rights and freedoms, an appropriate quality of life for citizens, sovereignty, territorial integrity and stable development of the Russian federation, the defense and security of the state;

—"national interests of the Russian Federation"—the aggregate of the internal and external needs of the state in ensuring the protection and stable development of the individual, society, and the state;

—"threat to national security"—the direct or indirect possibility of damage to constitutional rights and freedoms, quality of life, sovereignty/territorial integrity, stable development of the RF, defense and security of the state;

—"strategic national priorities"—the most important directions in terms of ensuring national security, in accordance with which are realized the constitutional rights and freedoms of RF citizens, stable socioeconomic development, and the protection of the country's sovereignty, independence and territorial integrity;

—"system of national security"—the forces and means which ensure national security;

—"forces of national security"—the Armed Forces of the Russian Federation, other troops, military formations and bodies which under federal legislation are designated as engaging in military and/or law enforcement service, and likewise federal organs of state power which participate in the provision of national security on the basis of legislation of the Russian Federation;

—"means of ensuring national security"— technologies, and likewise technical, programming, linguistic, legal, and organizational resources, including telecommunications channels, which are used within the system of provision of national security in order to collect, formulate, process, transmit or receive information on the status of national security and measures for its reinforcement.

7. The forces and means which ensure national security concentrate their efforts and resources on the provision of national security in the political, economic, and social spheres, in the areas of science and education, in the intercultural, spiritual, informational, military, military-industrial, and ecological spheres, and likewise in the area of social security.

II. RUSSIA AND THE MODERN WORLD: CURRENT CONDITIONS AND TRENDS OF DEVELOPMENT

8. World development is following the path of globalization in all spheres of international life, which, in turn, is characterized by a high degree of dynamism and interdependence of events.

Nation-states have experienced the intensification of conflicts connected to unequal development, as a result of globalizing processes, and of the deepening rift between rich and poor countries. Values and models of development have become the subject of global competition.

The vulnerability of all members of the international community to new threats and challenges has grown.

As a result of the rise of new centers of economic growth and political influence, a qualitatively new geopolitical situation is unfolding. There is an increasing tendency to seek resolutions to existing problems and regulate crisis situations on a regional basis, without the participation of non-regional powers.

The inadequacy of the current global and regional architecture, oriented (particularly in the Euro-Atlantic region) towards NATO, and likewise the imperfect nature of legal instruments and mechanisms, create an ever-increasing threat to international security.

9. The transition in the international system from opposing blocs to principles of multi-vector diplomacy, together with Russia's resource potential and pragmatic policy for its use, have broadened the possibilities for the Russian Federation to reinforce its influence on the world stage.

The Russian Federation has sufficient potential to count on the creation, in the medium-term, of conditions conducive to its entrenchment among the leaders of the world economy, on the basis of effective participation in global division of labor, improved global competitiveness of the national economy, of defense potential, and of the level of state and social security.

10. A negative influence on the assurance of Russia's national interests will be exerted by the likely recurrence of one-sided use of force in international relations, disagreements between the main participants in world politics, the threat of proliferation of weapons of mass destruction and of their use by terrorists, and likewise the improvement of forms of illicit activity in the cybernetic and biological domains, in the sphere of high technology. The global information struggle will intensify, threats will increase to the stability of industrialized and developing countries, their socio-economic development and democratic institutions. Nationalist sentiments, xenophobia, separatism, and violent extremism will grow, including under the banner of religious radicalism. The global demographic situation and environmental problems will become more acute, and threats associated with uncontrolled and illegal migration, drug and human trafficking, and other forms of transnational organized crime, will also increase. Epidemics caused by new, previously unknown viruses are likely to spread. The deficit of fresh water will become more obvious.

11.   In the long term, the attention of international politics will be focused on ownership of energy resources, including in the Near East, the Barents Sea shelf and other parts of the Arctic, in the Caspian basin, and in Central Asia.

In the medium term, the situation in Iraq and Afghanistan, as well as conflicts in the Near and Middle East, in a number of South Asian and African countries, and on the Korean peninsula, will continue to exert a negative influence on the international situation.

12.   The critical condition of physical storage of dangerous materials and objects, especially in countries with unstable political situations, together with the proliferation of regular armaments beyond the control of the state, can lead to the intensification of existing, as well as the creation of new regional and interstate conflicts.

Under conditions of competition for resources, it is not excluded that arising problems may be resolved using military force, and that the current balance of power on the borders of Russia and its allies may be disturbed.

There is an increasing risk that the number of countries possessing nuclear weapons will rise.

The possibility of maintaining global and regional stability will substantially decrease with the placement in Europe of elements of the global missile defense system of the United States of America.

The consequences of global financial-economic crises may become comparable, in terms of overall losses, to the consequences of large-scale application of military force.

13.   In the long term, the Russian Federation will seek to construct international relations based on the principles of international law, and on the institution of reliable and equal security of nation-states.

For the defense of its national interests, Russia, while remaining within the boundaries of international law, will implement a rational and pragmatic foreign policy, one that excludes expensive confrontation, including a new arms race.

Russia perceives the United Nations and the Security Council of the United Nations as a central element of a stable system of international relations, at the basis of which lie respect, equal rights, and mutually beneficial cooperation among nations, resting on civilized political instruments for the resolution of global and regional crisis situations.

Russia will increase its interaction with multilateral fora such as the G8, G20, RIC (Russia/India/China), BRIC (Brazil/Russia/India/China), and will likewise capitalize on the potential of other informal international institutions.

The development of bilateral and multilateral cooperation with member states of the Commonwealth of Independent States is a priority direction of Russian foreign policy. Russia will seek to develop the potential for regional and sub regional integration and coordination among member states of the CIS, first of all within the framework of the Commonwealth, and also the CSTO and EvrAzEs, which exert a stabilizing influence on the overall situation in the regions bordering on the CIS.

Moreover, the CSTO is regarded as the main interstate instrument for responding to regional threats and challenges of a military-political or military-strategic nature, including the fight with illegal trafficking in narcotic and psychotropic substances.

14. Russia will promote the strengthening of EvrAzEs as the nucleus of economic integration, and instrument of assistance to the realization of major hydropower, infrastructural, industrial and other joint projects having a primarily regional significance.

15. Of particular significance for Russia will be the reinforcement of the political potential of the SCO, and the stimulation within its framework of practical steps towards the enhancement of mutual trust and partnership in the Central Asian region.

16. The Russian Federation is in favor strengthening the mechanisms of cooperation with the European Union by all possible means, including the continued formation of common spaces in the economic, educational,

scientific and cultural spheres, and in terms of internal and external security. The long-term national interests of Russia are served by the creation of an open system of Euro-Atlantic collective security, on a clear legal and treaty basis.

17.   A determining aspect of relations with NATO remains the fact that plans to extend the alliance's military infrastructure to Russia's borders, and attempts to endow NATO with global functions that go counter to norms of international law, are unacceptable to Russia.

Russia is prepared to develop relations with NATO on the basis of equality and in the interests of strengthening the general security of the Euro-Atlantic region. The content and depth of these relations will be determined by the preparedness of the alliance to recognize Russia's legal interests when engaging in military-political planning, and to respect norms of international law; and likewise NATO's readiness to consider the further transformation of these relations and the search for new tasks and functions with a humanitarian orientation.

18.   Russia will strive to build an equitable and valuable strategic partnership with the United States of America, on the basis of shared interests and taking into account the key influence of Russian-American

relations on the international situation as a whole. In terms of priorities, these will continue to be the achievement of new agreements in the sphere of disarmament and arms control, the reinforcement of confidence building measures, and likewise the resolution of issues surrounding non-proliferation of weapons of mass destruction, the development of antiterrorist cooperation, and the regulation of regional conflicts.

19. In the sphere of international security, Russia will maintain its adherence to the use of political, legal, economic, military and other instruments to defend state sovereignty and national interests.

   The execution of a predictable and open foreign policy is inextricably tied to the realization of Russia's stable development. The successful integration of Russia into the global economic space and the international division of labor is inhibited by the slow pace of transition of the national economy towards an innovation-based development trajectory.

20. For the prevention of threats to national security, it is essential to guarantee social stability, ethnic and denominational harmony, increase the mobilization potential and growth of the national economy, as well as improve the quality of work performed by state bodies and formulate effective mechanisms for their

interaction with civil society, in order to realize the right of every Russian citizen to life, security, work, housing, health and a healthy way of life, accessible education, and cultural development.

III. NATIONAL INTERESTS OF THE RUSSIAN FEDERATION AND STRATEGIC NATIONAL PRIORITIES

21.   The national interests of the Russian Federation in the long term consist of the following:

—developing democracy and civil society, and the enhancement of the competitiveness of the national economy;

—ensuring the solidity of the constitutional system, territorial integrity, and sovereignty of the Russian Federation;

—transforming the Russian Federation into a world power, whose activity is directed at supporting the strategic stability and mutually beneficial partner relationships within the multi-polar world.

22.   The internal and external sovereign needs of the state with regards to ensuring national security are realized via the strategic national priorities.

23. The main national security priorities of the Russian Federation are national defense and state and social security.

24. In order to ensure national security, the Russian Federation, as well as achieving the basic priorities of national security, concentrates its efforts and resources on the following priorities of stable development:

—increasing the quality of life of Russian citizens by guaranteeing individual security, high standards of living, and economic growth which is achieved first and foremost by developing a national system of innovation and by investing in human capital; science, technology, education, healthcare, and culture, which are developed by reinforcing the role of the state and improving public-private partnership;

—ecology of living systems and rational resource use, supported by balanced consumption, development of progressive technologies, and expedient use of the country's resources;

—strategic stability and equitable strategic partnership, on the basis of Russia's active participation in the development of the multi-polar model of the international system.

IV. ENSURING NATIONAL SECURITY

25.   The main components of the provision of national
security consist of the maintenance of legal and insti-
tutional mechanisms, and likewise of the resources of
the state and society, at a level corresponding to the
national interests of the Russian Federation.

The state of national security of the Russian
Federation is directly dependent on the economic
potential of the country and the effectiveness of the
system of provision of national security.

1. NATIONAL DEFENSE

26.   The strategic goals related to improving national
defense consist of preventing global and regional wars
and conflicts, and likewise of realizing strategic deterrence in the interests of ensuring the country's military
security.

Strategic deterrence presupposes the development
and systemic realization of a range of interconnected
political, diplomatic, military, economic, informational,
and other measures, intended to forestall or reduce the
threat of destructive action on the part of a state
aggressor (coalition of states).

Strategic deterrence is realized with the use of the
state's economic resources, including support for the
forces providing national security, by means of the

development of a system of military-patriotic education of Russian citizens and likewise of military infrastructure and administration systems for the state military organization.

27.   The Russian Federation provides national defense on the basis of principles of reasonable sufficiency and effectiveness, including by means of non-military response, mechanisms of public diplomacy and peace-keeping, and international military cooperation.

28.   Military security is ensured by developing and improving the military organization and defensive potential of the state and likewise the allocation of sufficient financial, material, and other resources for this purpose.

      The strategic objectives of national defense are realized by developing the system of national security, implementing a long-term military-technological policy and developing military infrastructure, and likewise by improving the system of administration of the state military organization and by realizing a range of measures increasing the prestige of military service.

29.   The long-term state policy of the Russian Federation in the area of national defense and military construction, including within the framework of the Union State [with Belarus], is oriented towards the improvement of the Armed Forces of the Russian Federation,

other troops, military formations and bodies, called upon to ensure the security, sovereignty, and territorial integrity of the state, under any given conditions of the military-political environment.

30.   Threats to military security include the policies of a number of leading foreign countries, directed at achieving predominant superiority in the military sphere, primarily in terms of strategic nuclear forces, but also by developing high-precision, informational, and other high-technology means of conducting armed warfare, strategic non-nuclear arms, by unilaterally creating a global missile defense system and militarizing space, which could lead to a new arms race, and likewise policies directed at the proliferation of nuclear, chemical, and biological technologies, and the production of weapons of mass destruction, their delivery systems, or their components.

Negative influences on the military security of the Russian Federation and its allies are aggravated by the departure from international agreements pertaining to arms limitation and reduction, and likewise by actions intended to disrupt the stability of systems of government and military administration, rocket attack warning systems, control of outer space, the functioning of strategic nuclear forces, nuclear weapons storage facilities, nuclear energy, nuclear and chemical industry, and other potentially dangerous sites.

31.   The Russian Federation realizes the long-term state policy of national defense by developing a system of foundational conceptual documents, and likewise of documents concerned with planning and developing norms of legal regulation of state bodies, of institutions, of enterprises and organizations of the real economy, and of civil society institutions, in times of peace and war; and, moreover, with the improvement of the forces and means of civil defense, as well as the country's communication networks and transport infrastructure in the interests of national defense.

32.   The main challenge of strengthening national defense in the medium term is the transition towards a qualitatively new profile for the Armed Forces of the Russian Federation, while maintaining the potential of the strategic nuclear forces, by improving the organizational staff structure and system of territorially-based troops and forces, increasing the number of divisions at constant readiness, and likewise improving operations and combat training, as well as improving the organization of interaction among different troops and forces.

To this end, the recruitment system of the Armed Forces of the Russian Federation, other troops, military formations and bodies is being clarified, including personnel training and development of relevant infrastructure; optimal standby mechanisms are being developed; the prestige of military service and officers' status is being enhanced; and likewise government programs and contracts are being executed for the development, creation, and modernization of arms, military and specialist technology, including means of communication, reconnaissance, electronic warfare, and command control.

33.   In the medium term, the transition towards a single system of contracts by the federal organs of executive power for armaments, military and specialist technology to supply the Armed Forces of the Russian Federation, other troops, military formations and bodies, should be completed, as should the transition to a unified system of logistics and technical support. Normative legal regulation of the maintenance of supplies of material resources in the state- and mobilization reserve should be achieved and likewise the collaboration with other states in the area of military security.

34.   The restructuring, optimization and development of the military-industrial complex of the Russian Federation in the medium term corresponds to the resolution of challenges regarding the comprehensive and timely provision of modern armaments and specialized technology to the Armed Forces of the Russian Federation, other troops, military formations and bodies.

2. STATE AND PUBLIC SECURITY

35. Strategic national security objectives in the sphere of state and public security are the protection of Russia's constitutional system, of the basic rights and freedoms of the individual and the citizen, of the sovereignty, independence and territorial integrity of the Russian Federation, and likewise the preservation of civil peace, political and social stability.

36. For the provision of national security in the domain of long-term state and public security, the Russian Federation starts from the necessity of constant improvements to law enforcement measures for the exposure, prevention, disruption, and discovery of acts of terrorism, extremism, and other criminal infringements on the rights and freedoms of the individual and the citizen, on property, on social order and public security, and on the constitutional system of the Russian Federation.

37. The main threats to national security in the sphere of state and public security are as follows:

—investigative or other activity by the special services and organizations of foreign countries and likewise by individual persons, directed at causing harm to the security of the Russian Federation;

—the activity of terrorist organizations, groups and individuals, directed at violent changes to the constitutional system of the Russian Federation, the disruption of normal functioning of state bodies (including violent action against governmental, political and social actors), the destruction of military or industrial sites, enterprises and institutions providing for vital social activities, and intimidation of the population, including by means of nuclear and chemical weapons or dangerous radioactive, chemical, and biological substances;

—the extremist activity of nationalist, religious, ethnic or other organizations and structures, directed at destroying the unity and territorial integrity of the Russian Federation, destabilization of the internal political and social situation in the country;

—the activity of transnational criminal organizations and groupings, connected to illegal trafficking of narcotic and psychotropic substances, weapons, ammunition, and explosive substances;

—the persistent growth of criminal acts, directed against the individual, property, state power, public and economic security, and likewise acts connected to corruption.

38.   The main long-term directions of state policy in the
        sphere of state and public security must be the rein-
        forcement of the role of the state as guarantor of the
        security of the individual, first of all children and ado-
        lescents; the improvement of normative legal regula-
        tion of the fight against and prevention of criminality,
        corruption, terrorism, and extremism; more effective
        defense of the rights and lawful interests of Russian
        citizens abroad; and the expansion of global collabora-
        tion in law enforcement.

39.   Long-term state and public security will likewise be
        supported by the increased effectiveness of law-
        enforcement organs and special services, by the cre-
        ation of a single state system for the prevention of
        criminality (first of all concerning minors) and of other
        unlawful acts, a system which will encompass moni-
        toring and evaluating the effectiveness of law enforce-
        ment practices, and developing and applying special
        measures directed at reducing the level of corruption
        and criminalization of social relations.

40.   In order to ensure state and public security:

        —the structures and activity of federal organs of
        executive power are being improved, a National
        Anticorruption Plan is being implemented, a system of
        discovery and response to the global threats and crises
        of modernity is being developed, including international

and national terrorism, political and religious extremism, nationalism and ethnic separatism;

—mechanisms for the forecasting and neutralization of social and interethnic conflicts are being created;

—a long-term concept for the comprehensive development and improvement of law-enforcement organs and special services is being formulated, social guarantees for their employees are being strengthened, scientific-technical support for law enforcement activity is being improved, promising specialist means and technologies are being adopted, a system of professional cadre training is being developed in the area of state and public security;

—a regime of secure functioning of the enterprises, organizations and institutions belonging to the country's military-industrial, nuclear, chemical, and nuclear energy complexes, and likewise of essential support systems for the life of the population;

—the social responsibility of bodies providing state and public security is being increased.

41. One of the conditions of national security is the reliable defense and protection of the state borders of the Russian Federation.

The main threats to the border-related interests and security of the Russian Federation are the presence and possible escalation of armed conflicts near its state borders, the Security threats to borders include the activity of international terrorist and extremist organizations which base their emissaries and terrorist means in Russia and organize sabotage on Russian territory, and likewise the increased activity of transnational criminal groupings engaged in the illegal transfer across the Russian border of narcotic and psychotropic substances, goods and cargo, water and biological resources, other material and cultural valuables, and in the organization of channels for illegal migration.

A negative effect on the reliable defense and protection of Russia's state borders is exerted by the insufficient level of development of border infrastructure and of technological equipment for border-related bodies.

42.   The resolution of border security problems is achieved by creating high-tech and multifunctional border complexes, particularly on the borders with the Republic of Kazakhstan, Ukraine, Georgia, and Azerbaijan, and likewise by increasing the effectiveness of state border defense, particularly in the Arctic zone of the Russian Federation, the Far East, and on the Caspian.

43.   The provision of national security in emergency situations is achieved by improving and developing a single public warning and relief system for emergency situations of both a natural and man-made character

(comprising territorial and functional segments) and integrating it with analogous systems abroad.

The resolution of national security challenges in emergency situations is achieved by increasing the effective implementation of the powers of local self-government bodies pertaining to the security of the population's vital activities, renewing technological equipment and the technologies of production at potentially dangerous sites and essential facilities, introducing modern technological means of informing and notifying the population in public places, and likewise developing systems of preventative measures to lower the risk of terrorist acts and allay the consequences of emergency situations of a man-made or natural character.

44.   The Russian Federation is strengthening national defense and providing state and public security with the goal of creating internal and external conditions favorable to the achievement of socioeconomic development priorities.

3. IMPROVEMENT OF THE QUALITY OF LIFE OF RUSSIAN CITIZENS

45.   The strategic goals in terms of ensuring national security in the area of improving the quality of life of Russian citizens are the reduction of social and material inequalities within the population, the stabilization of

population size in the medium term, and in the long term—the fundamental improvement of the demographic situation.

46.   The improvement of the quality of life of Russian citizens is guaranteed by ensuring individual security and likewise access to comfortable housing, safe and high quality goods and services, and a dignified wage for active labor.

47.   Sources of threats to national security could include factors such as a crisis within global and regional financial-banking systems, an intensification of competition over insufficient raw materials, energy, water and food resources, or a lag in the development of cutting-edge technologies, which increase strategic risks associated with dependence on changes in external factors.

48.   National security in the domain of improving the quality of life of Russian citizens will be supported by the reduction of organized crime, corruption, and drug addiction; by preventing organized criminal groups from legalizing their economic activities; by achieving sociopolitical stability and a positive dynamic of development of the Russian Federation, as well as the ensuring the stability of the financial-banking system, broader exploitation of mineral and raw material resources, accessibility of modern education and

healthcare, high social mobility and support for socially significant labor activity, superior qualifications and quality of labor resources, and finally the rational organization of migratory flows.

49.   One of the main elements of ensuring national security in the medium term includes food security and the guaranteed provision of high-quality, accessible medications.

50.   Food security is assured by developing biotechnologies and import-substitution of basic food products, as well as by preventing soil depletion, the reduction of agricultural and arable land, the capture of domestic grain markets by foreign companies, and the uncontrolled dissemination of food products made from genetically modified plants, with the use of genetically modified microorganisms and microorganisms having genetically modified analogues.

51.   In the interests of developing the pharmaceutical sector, conditions are being created to overcome its dependence on foreign suppliers for raw materials.

52.   In order to counteract threats to national security with regards to the quality of life of Russian citizens, the forces of national security together with civil society institutions:

—improve the national system of human rights protection by developing an appropriate legal system and legislation;

—assist the growth of well-being, the reduction of poverty and of income disparities with the goal of ensuring continuous access of all citizens to a quantity of food products essential to a healthy lifestyle;

—create the conditions necessary for living a healthy lifestyle, stimulate birth rates, and lower death rates;

—improve and develop transport infrastructure, increase protection of the population from emergency situations of both natural and man-made origins;

—ensure the preservation of a cultural and spiritual legacy, the accessibility of information technologies, and likewise of information on various issues of the sociopolitical, economic, and spiritual life of society;

—improve public-private partnership with the goal of strengthening the material-technical base of healthcare, cultural and educational institutions, of developing residential construction projects, and enhancing the quality of housing and community services.

4. ECONOMIC GROWTH

53.   Strategic national security objectives include Russia's
       entry, in the medium term, into the ranks of the top
       five countries by size of GDP and likewise the achieve-
       ment of the necessary degree of national security in the
       economic and technological spheres.

54.   The provision of national security by means of eco-
       nomic growth is achieved by developing a national
       system of innovation, increasing the productivity of
       labor, acquiring new resources, modernizing priority
       sectors of the national economy, and improving the
       banking system, the financial services sector, and inter-
       governmental fiscal relations in the Russian Federation.

55.   The main long-term strategic risks and threats to
       national security in the economic sphere are the main-
       tenance of a raw materials export model of economic
       development, the lessening of competitiveness and the
       high dependence on external economic conditions, the
       loss of control over national resources, the worsening
       of the condition of the industrial and energy resource
       base, the unequal development of the regions and pro-
       gressive labor shortages, the low levels of stability and
       protection of the national financial system, the persis-
       tence of conditions conducive to the corruption and
       criminalization of economic and financial relation-
       ships, and also to illegal migration.

56. The insufficient effectiveness of state regulation of the national economy, falling economic growth rates, the appearance of trade and balance of payment deficits, the contraction of budget revenues could lead to delays in the transition to innovation-based growth, and to the consequent accumulation of social problems in the country.

57. A direct negative effect on national security in the economic sphere may be exerted by a deficit of fuel-energy, water, and biological resources, by the adoption of discriminatory measures and the intensification of unfair competition with regards to Russia, and likewise due to crisis phenomena in the global financial-banking system.

58. For the provision of national security by means of economic growth, the Russian Federation is concentrating its main efforts on the development of science, technology, and education, and on the improvement of national investment and financial institutions, in the interests of achieving an essential level of security in the military, military-industrial, and international spheres.

59. Threats to national security related to disproportional levels of development among subjects of the Russian Federation are prevented by means of a rational regional policy directed at the improved coordination

of state bodies, local administrations, the business community, and civil society.

60.   One of the main long-term directions of national security in the economic sphere is energy security. Essential conditions of national and global energy security include multilateral cooperation in the interests of creating markets for energy resources that correspond to WTO principles, the development and international exchange of promising energy-saving technologies and likewise the use of ecologically clean, alternative sources of energy.

The main aspects of energy security are the stable supply of sufficient standard quality sources of energy; the effective use of energy resources by increasing the competitiveness of domestic producers; the prevention of possible fuel-energy resource deficits; the creation of strategic stocks of fuel, reserve capacities, and standard equipment; and ensuring the stable functioning of the system of energy and fuel provision.

61.   In order to counteract threats to economic security, the forces of national security in cooperation with civil society institutions aim to support state socioeconomic policy, which is directed at:

—perfecting structures of production and export, antimonopoly regulation, and support for competition policy;

—developing a national system of innovation with the goal of implementing highly effective projects and priority programs developing the high-technology economic sectors;

—strengthening financial markets and increasing the liquidity of the banking system;

—reducing the informal sector and legalizing labor relations, increasing investment in the development of human capital;

—balancing the interests of the indigenous population with those of migrant laborers, taking into account their ethnic, linguistic, cultural, and denominational differences, including by improving migration records and likewise by ensuring the fair territorial distribution of migrant labor based on the labor resource requirements of the regions;

—establishing a system of scientific and technical forecasting and implementing scientific and technical priorities, intensifying the integration of science, education, and industry;

—creating conditions for the development of a competitive domestic pharmaceutical industry;

—developing the industries of information and telecommunication technologies, computer technology resources, electronics, telecommunications equipment, and programming.

62.   In the interests of ensuring national security in the medium term, competitive economic sectors are being developed and markets for Russian products are being expanded, the effectiveness of the fuel-energy complex is being enhanced, instruments of public-private partnership are being used to resolve strategic challenges to economic development and to the completion of a basic transport, energy, information, and military infrastructure, especially in the Arctic zone, Eastern Siberia, and the Far East of the Russian Federation.

63.   The strengthening of economic security will be supported by the improvement of state regulation of economic growth, by developing conceptual and programmatic documents of interregional and territorial planning, and creating a comprehensive system of risk control, including:

—introduction of an active state anti-inflation, currency, exchange rate, and monetary-credit and taxation-budgetary policy, aimed at import-substitution and supporting the real economy;

—stimulation and support for the development of a market for innovation, high-tech production, and high value-added production, and the development of promising general-, dual-, and special-purpose technologies.

64.   At the regional level, the stable condition of national security is ensured by the balanced, comprehensive and systemic development of the subjects of the Russian Federation.

One of the main medium-term directions of national security at the regional level is the creation of mechanisms intended to reduce the level of interregional disparity in the socioeconomic development of the subjects of the Russian Federation, by means of balanced territorial development.

In the long term, threats to national security related to the disproportionate levels of development of the Russian regions are prevented by launching a full-scale national innovation system, by creating territorial-industrial areas in the southern regions and Middle Volga, in the Ural region and in Siberia, in the Far East, and in other regions of the Russian Federation.

65.   In order to achieve regional development, the forces of national security in cooperation with civil society

institutions support the effective implementation of the powers of state bodies of the subjects of the Russian Federation and local self-governing bodies, by coordinating and implementing measures taken at the federal, regional, and municipal levels, directed at the development of the regional economic and social sphere, including the equalization of their budgetary provisions.

5. SCIENCE, TECHNOLOGY, AND EDUCATION

66. Strategic national security goals in the sphere of science, technology, and education are as follows:

—developing state scientific and scientific-technical organizations, capable of providing competitive advantages for the national economy and the needs of national defense, by means of effective coordination of scientific research and the development of a national system of innovation;

—increasing social mobility, the population's general and professional level of education, and the professional qualities of highly qualified cadres, by means of the accessibility of competitive education.

67. A direct negative effect on national security in terms of science, technology, and education is caused by the country falling behind in the transition towards the next technological order, by dependence on imported

deliveries of scientific equipment, instruments, electronic components, and strategic materials, by the unsanctioned transfer abroad of competitive domestic technologies, by unfounded unilateral sanctions against Russia's scientific and educational institutions, by the insufficient development of the normative legal base and weak motivation to formulate policies around innovation and industry, by the low level of social protection for engineering-technical, professorial, and pedagogical, the low quality of general secondary education and of professional primary, secondary, and higher education.

68. One of the main policy directions of the Russian Federation in the medium term is determined by technological security. To this end, a state policy pertaining to industry and innovation is being perfected; fundamental and applied research, together with education, are defined as unquestionable priorities of the innovational development of the national economy; a system of federal and public contracts for the training of highly qualified specialists and workers is being improved; public-private partnerships are being developed in science and technology; conditions are being created for the integration of science, education, and industry; systemic research is being conducted in the interests of resolving strategic challenges of national defense, state and public security, and likewise of the country's stable development.

69. In order to counteract threats in the spheres of science, technology, and education, the forces of national security in cooperation with civil society institutions implement the civil education of new generations in the traditions of the prestige of the scientist and the pedagogue, ensure the effectiveness of state regulation in relation to integrating science, education, and high-technological industry.

70. The resolution of national security issues in the area of science, technology, and education in the medium- and long-term are achieved by the following means:

—formulating systems of targeted fundamental and applied research and their support by the state in the interests of an organizational-scientific approach to achieving strategic national priorities;

—creating a network of federal universities and national research universities that would ensure, within a framework of cooperative relationships, the training of specialists for work in science and education, the development of competitive technologies and exemplary high-tech production, and the organization of high-tech production;

—implementing programs establishing institutions of learning oriented at training cadres to serve the needs of regional development, as well as the organs and forces of national security;

—ensuring the participation of Russian scientific and scientific-educational organizations in global technological and research projects, taking into account the state of the intellectual property market.

6. HEALTHCARE

71. Strategic national security goals in the area of healthcare and the health of the nation are as follows:

—increasing life expectancy, reducing disability and mortality;

—improving disease prevention and the provision of timely, qualified primary healthcare and high-technology medical assistance;

—improving standards of medical assistance and likewise of the quality, as well as effectiveness and safety of medicines.

72. One of the main threats to national security in terms of healthcare and national health is the appearance of large-scale epidemics and pandemics, the mass spread of HIV infection, tuberculosis, drug addiction, alcoholism, and

the increased accessibility of psychoactive and psychotropic substances.

73.   A direct negative effect on national security in the
       domain of healthcare and the health of the nation is
       exerted by the low effectiveness of the medical insur-
       ance system and the low quality of health-care special-
       ist training and retraining; the insufficient level of
       social guarantees and wages for medical workers and
       insufficient financing for the system of high-technology
       medical assistance; the incomplete formation of a nor-
       mative legal basis for healthcare oriented at increasing
       accessibility and implementing guarantees of medical
       assistance for the general population.

74.   The state policy of the Russian Federation relating to
       healthcare and the health of the nation is geared at
       preventive medicine and also at preventing the spread
       of socially dangerous illnesses.

75.   The main directions of national security policy in the
       sphere of healthcare and national health of the Russian
       Federation are determined in the medium term by the
       intensification of the preventative orientation of
       healthcare, focusing on preserving human health, and
       preserving the institution of the family, motherhood,
       fatherhood and childhood, as the foundations of social
       vitality.

76.   The strengthening of national security in the area of
       healthcare and national health will be supported by
       enhancing the quality and accessibility of medical ser-
       vices, by using promising information and telecom-
       munications technologies, by means of state support
       for promising pharmaceutical, biotechnological, and
       nano-technological research, and likewise by modern-
       izing economic mechanisms involved in the functioning
       of healthcare and developing the material-technical
       base of state and municipal health-care systems, taking
       regional particularities into consideration.

77.   In order to counteract threats to healthcare and the
       health of the nation, the forces of national security in
       cooperation with civil society institutions ensure the
       effectiveness of state regulation in the area of stan-
       dardization, licensing, and certification of medical
       services, in the accreditation of medical and pharma-
       ceutical establishments, in the provision of state guar-
       antees for receiving medical assistance and
       modernizing the system of obligatory medical insur-
       ance, and in the definition of uniform criteria evaluat-
       ing the work of centers for treatment and prevention
       at the level of municipal formations and subjects of
       the Russian Federation.

78.   The resolution of problems of national security in the
       sphere of healthcare and the health of the nation in the

medium and long term is achieved by the following means:

—formulating national programs (projects) for the treatment of socially significant diseases (oncological, cardiac-arterial, diabetic, and physiological illnesses, drug addiction, alcoholism) alongside the development of uniform approaches to the diagnosis, treatment, and rehabilitation of patients;

—developing an administrative system overseeing the quality and accessibility of medical assistance, and the training of health-care specialists;

—providing for the qualitative transformation of the structure of infections and for the liquidation of the preconditions of epidemics, including epidemics caused by particularly dangerous infectious pathogens, by developing and implementing promising technologies and national programs of state support for disease prevention.

7. CULTURE

79.   Strategic objectives ensuring national security in the cultural sphere are as follows:

—broadening access of large sections of the population to the best examples of national and foreign culture and art by creating modern territorially distributed information banks;

—creating conditions for the stimulation of creative self-realization within the population, by improving systems of cultural enlightenment, the organization of leisure activities, and mass extracurricular artistic education;

—assisting the development of the cultural potential of Russia's regions and supporting regional cultural initiatives.

80. The main threats to national security in the cultural sphere are the dominance of production of mass culture oriented towards the spiritual needs of marginalized groups and likewise unlawful infringements against cultural objects.

81. Negative influences on the state of national security in the cultural sphere are intensified by attempts to revise perspectives on Russia's history, its role, and its place in world history; and by the propagandizing of a lifestyle based on permissiveness and violence, or racial, national, and religious intolerance.

82. In order to counteract threats in the cultural sphere, the forces of national security together with civil society institutions ensure the effectiveness of state regulation

intended to support and develop national cultures, tolerance, self-respect, and likewise the development of international [in the sense of interethnic] and interregional cultural ties.

83.   The strengthening of national security in the cultural sphere will be served by preserving and developing indigenous cultures within Russia's multinational population, and the citizenry's spiritual values; by improving the material-technical basis of cultural and leisure establishments; by perfecting the system of training of cadres and providing for their social welfare; by supporting the production and distribution of domestic cinematography; by developing cultural tourism; by establishing government contracts for the creation of cinematographic and printed works, television, radio programs, and internet resources; and likewise by using Russia's cultural potential in the service of multilateral international cooperation.

84.   In the medium and long term, the resolution of national security challenges in the cultural sphere are achieved by acknowledging the primary role of culture in the rebirth and preservation of cultural-moral values, by reinforcing the spiritual unity of the multinational population of the Russian Federation and the international image of Russia as a country with a very rich traditional and dynamically developing contemporary culture, by creating a system of spiritual and

patriotic education for Russian citizens, and finally by
developing.

8. THE ECOLOGY OF LIVING SYSTEMS
AND ENVIRONMENTAL MANAGEMENT

85.   Strategic objectives relating to ecological security and
environmental management are:

—preserving of the environment and ensuring its
protection;

—redressing the environmental consequences of
economic activity in the context of a growing economy
and global climate changes.

86.   The state of national security in the ecological sphere
is negatively affected by the depletion of world reserves
of mineral, water and biological resources, and likewise by the presence in the Russian Federation of ecologically disadvantaged regions.

87.   The state of national security in the ecological sphere
is worsened by the maintenance of a significant number of dangerous production processes, whose activity
leads to the destruction of the ecological balance,
including the disruption of sanitary-epidemiological
and/or sanitary-hygienic standards of drinking water
used by the general population; disposal of radioactive

waste from the nuclear fuel cycle is not subject to normative legal regulation and oversight. The strategic risk of exhaustion of the country's most important mineral and raw material resources is growing, as the rate of extraction of many mineral resources declines.

88.   In order to counteract threats in the sphere of ecological security and environmental management, the forces of national security together with civil society institutions create the conditions for the introduction of ecologically safe production; the search for promising energy sources; the creation and implementation of a state program for the establishment of strategic reserves of mineral and raw material resources sufficient to supply Russia's mobilization requirements; and the guaranteed provision of water and biological resources to meet the needs of the population and the economy.

9. STRATEGIC STABILITY AND EQUITABLE STRATEGIC PARTNERSHIP

89.   The achievement of the Russian Federation's priorities for stable development is supported by an active foreign policy, whose efforts are focused on seeking agreement and common interests with other states, on the basis of a system of bilateral and multilateral mutually beneficial partnership relations.

90.   The creation of favorable conditions for Russia's stable
       development in the long term is achieved by ensuring
       strategic stability, including by means of consistent
       movement towards a world free from nuclear weapons,
       and by creating conditions of equal security for all.

91.   Russia bases its relations with the international com-
       munity on the principle of maintaining stability and
       predictability in the area of strategic offensive arms and
       attributes particular significance to the achievement of
       new full-scale bilateral agreements on the continued
       reduction and limitation of strategic offensive arms.

92.   Russia will assist with engaging other states, first of all
       those possessing nuclear weapons but also those inter-
       ested in joint action to ensure mutual security, in a
       process of establishing strategic stability.

93.   Russia believes that the maintenance of strategic stabil-
       ity and equitable strategic partnership can be sup-
       ported by the presence of contingents of the Armed
       Forces of the Russian Federation in conflict zones, on
       the basis of norms of international law, with the goal
       of resolving political, economic, and other challenges
       by non-military means.

94.   On the world stage, Russia will act from a position
       founded on an unchanging course towards joint

participation with other states in the reinforcement of
international mechanisms for nonproliferation of
nuclear weapons and other weapons of mass destruction, means of their delivery, and related goods and
technologies; on the unacceptability of use of military
force in contravention of the United Nations Charter;
and likewise from a position of adherence to arms
control and rational sufficiency in military construction.

95.   In order to preserve strategic stability and equitable
strategic partnership, the Russian Federation:

—will fulfill existing treaties and agreements pertaining
to the limitation and reduction of arms, will participate
in the development and conclusion of new agreements
corresponding to Russia's national interests;

—is prepared to engage in further discussion of
questions surrounding the reduction of nuclear
potentials on the basis of bilateral agreements and in
multilateral fora and likewise will assist in creating
appropriate conditions, allowing for the reduction
of nuclear armaments without detracting from
international security or strategic stability;

—intends to continue assisting the reinforcement of
regional stability by means of participation in processes
of reduction and limitation of ordinary armed forces

and likewise the development and application of confidence building measures in the military domain;

—considers international peacekeeping to be a viable instrument for the resolution of armed conflicts, stands for strengthening this institution in strict accordance with the principles of the United Nations Charter, and will continue its participation therein;

—will participate in efforts led by the UN and other international organizations to relieve natural and man-made catastrophes and crisis situations and likewise in the provision of humanitarian assistance to affected countries.

96. In the interests of strategic stability and equitable multilateral interaction on the international stage, during the period of realization of this Strategy Russia will undertake all necessary efforts, with minimum expenditure, to maintain parity with the United States of America in the area of strategic offensive arms, given a situation in which the United States of America is unfolding a global missile defense system and implementing a global "lightning strike" concept using nuclear- and non-nuclear-equipped strategic bombers.

V. ORGANIZATIONAL, LEGAL-NORMATIVE AND INFORMATIONAL FOUNDATIONS OF THE REALIZATION OF THE GIVEN STRATEGY

97. The state policy of the Russian Federation in the area of national security is the result of the concerted effort of all elements of the system providing national security, with a coordinating role being played by the Security Council of the Russian Federation with respect to the realization of a range of measures of an organizational, legal-normative, and informational nature.

98. The realization of the given strategy is ensured by the consolidation of the energies and resources of state bodies and civil society institutions, directed towards the defense of Russia's national interests by means of political, organizational, socioeconomic, legal, special, and other measures, developed within the framework of strategic planning in the Russian Federation.

99. Periodic amendments to the given Strategy are realized under the aegis of the Security Council of the Russian Federation — in accordance with the results of the constant monitoring of the realization of the given Strategy and in view of developments that would have a substantial influence on the state of national security.

100.   Organizational support for the realization of the given Strategy consists of the improvement of the public administration of the Russian Federation and likewise the development of a system of national security on the basis of improvements to strategic planning mechanisms geared at the stable development of the Russian Federation and at the provision of national security under the direction of the President of the Russian Federation.

101.   The system of documents of strategic planning (including the Concept of long-term socioeconomic development of the Russian Federation; the Program of short-term socioeconomic development of the Russian Federation; the strategies (programs) of development of separate economic sectors; the strategies (concepts) of development of the federal regions; the strategies and comprehensive programs of socioeconomic development of subjects of the Russian Federation; interstate programs in which Russia participates; federal (departmental) special programs; state defense contracting; conceptions, doctrines, and foundations (fundamental directions) of state policy with regards to ensuring national security and with regards to the domestic and foreign policy of the state) are formulated by the Government of the Russian Federation and relevant federal organs of executive power, with the participation of state bodies of the subjects of the Russian Federation, on the basis

of the Constitution of the Russian Federation, federal laws, and other normative legal acts of the Russian Federation.

102. By resolution of the president of the Russian Federation, documents regarding issues of domestic and foreign policy can be brought up for review before the Security Council of the Russian Federation.

103. The development of strategic planning documents is executed in agreement with the order of business [parliamentary procedure] of the government of the Russian Federation, and in accordance with the system of document preparation of the presidential administration of the Russian Federation.

104. State policy relating to the fight against terrorism and drug-related crimes is formulated by the State Antinarcotics Committee and the National Antiterrorism Committee—interdepartmental bodies which ensure coordination between federal organs of executive power and government bodies of the subjects of the Russian Federation in the relevant domains.

105. Comprehensive questions pertaining to national security may be examined at joint sessions of the Security Council of the Russian Federation, the State Council of the Russian Federation, and the Civic Chamber of the Russian Federation, with the participation of other

advisory and consultative bodies, created to guarantee the constitutional powers of the president of the Russian Federation.

106.   Normative legal measures supporting the realization of the given Strategy are determined on the basis of the Constitution of the Russian Federation, federal constitutional laws, federal laws, decrees and orders of the president of the Russian Federation, resolutions and acts of the Parliament of the Russian Federation, and likewise normative legal acts of the federal organs of executive power.

107.   The informational and informational-analytical support for the realization of the given Strategy is performed under the coordinating aegis of the Security Council of the Russian Federation, by attracting the information resources of relevant state bodies and state scientific institutions, with the use of a system of "distributed Situation Centers" working in coordination with one another.

108.   For the development of a system of Situation Centers in the medium term, it will be necessary to overcome technological lag in the most important areas of IT, telecommunications, and interconnectivity, which determine the state of national security; to develop and introduce technologies of information security into systems of government and military administration,

systems of management of ecologically dangerous products and critically important sites and likewise to create conditions for the harmonization of the national information infrastructure with global information networks and systems.

109.   Threats to information security in the course of realizing the given Strategy are prevented by improving the security of the information and telecommunications systems of critically important infrastructure and high-risk facilities in the Russian Federation; by increasing the level of protection of corporate and individual information systems; and by creating a unified system of information-telecommunication support for the system of national security.

110.   The development and realization of a range of efficient and prolonged measures for the prevention of threats to national security in the federal regions are performed by the federal organs of executive power in cooperation with the state bodies of the subjects of the Russian Federation, under the coordinating aegis of the government of the Russian Federation.

111.   Monitoring of the realization of the given Strategy is conducted within the framework of the annual report of the secretary of the Security Council of the Russian Federation to the president of the Russian Federation, regarding the state of national security and measures for its reinforcement.

VI. THE MAIN INDICATORS OF THE STATE OF NATIONAL SECURITY

112.   The main indicators of the state of national security are designated in order to evaluate the level of national security and include:

—the level of unemployment (as a proportion of the economically active population);

—the decile coefficient (the correlation between the incomes of the top and bottom 10% of the population);

—the rate of growth of consumer prices;

—the level of the internal and external state debt as a percentage of GDP;

—the level of fiscal support for health, culture, education and science as a percentage of GDP;

—the level of annual renewal of armaments and military and specialist equipment;

—the level of supply of military and engineering-technical cadres;

The list of basic indicators of national security can be made more precise in accordance with the results of monitoring of the state of national security.

The realization of the National Security Strategy of the Russian Federation to 2020 is expected to become a motivating factor in the development of the national economy; the improvement of the population's quality of life; the assurance of political stability within society; the reinforcement of national defense, state security, and law and order; and the enhancement of the competitiveness and international status of the Russian Federation.

INDEX